Google Cloud Platform Administration

Design highly available, scalable, and secure cloud solutions on GCP

Ranjit Singh Thakurratan

BIRMINGHAM - MUMBAI

Google Cloud Platform Administration

Copyright © 2018 Packt Publishing

Commissioning Editor: Vijin Boricha
Acquisition Editor: Prachi Bisht
Content Development Editor: Arjun Joshi
Technical Editor: Sayali Thanekar
Copy Editor: Safis Editing
Project Coordinator: Kinjal Bari
Proofreader: Safis Editing
Indexer: Pratik Shirodkar
Graphics: Jisha Chirayil
Production Coordinator: Arvindkumar Gupta

First published: September 2018

Production reference: 1290918

Published by Packt Publishing Ltd.
Livery Place
35 Livery Street
Birmingham
B3 2PB, UK.

ISBN 978-1-78862-435-0

www.packtpub.com

Made possible because of my wife Monica and my Pup Shyla....

`mapt.io`

Mapt is an online digital library that gives you full access to over 5,000 books and videos, as well as industry leading tools to help you plan your personal development and advance your career. For more information, please visit our website.

Why subscribe?

- Spend less time learning and more time coding with practical eBooks and Videos from over 4,000 industry professionals

- Improve your learning with Skill Plans built especially for you

- Get a free eBook or video every month

- Mapt is fully searchable

- Copy and paste, print, and bookmark content

Packt.com

Did you know that Packt offers eBook versions of every book published, with PDF and ePub files available? You can upgrade to the eBook version at `www.packt.com` and as a print book customer, you are entitled to a discount on the eBook copy. Get in touch with us at `customercare@packtpub.com` for more details.

At `www.packt.com`, you can also read a collection of free technical articles, sign up for a range of free newsletters, and receive exclusive discounts and offers on Packt books and eBooks.

Contributors

About the author

Ranjit Singh Thakurratan is a two-time published author and has over 10 years of multi-cloud expertise and works as a Principal Chief Architect at DellEMC. Ranjit holds a master's degree in Information Technology—infrastructure assurance and an engineering degree in computer science. He has presented at numerous conferences held at Boston, Washington DC, New York, Denver, and Dallas. He runs a technology blog and he can be reached via his Twitter handle, `@RJAPPROVES` and on Linkedin at `RJApproves`. Apart from technology, Ranjit is also interested in astrophysics, animal welfare, and open source projects.

About the reviewer

Chirag Nayyar helps organizations initiate their digital transformation using the public cloud. He has been actively working on cloud platforms since 2013, providing consultancy to many organizations ranging from small businesses to enterprises. He holds a wide range of certifications from all major public cloud platforms. He also runs meetups and is a regular speaker at various cloud events. He has also reviewed *Hands-On Machine Learning on Google Cloud Platform* and *Google Cloud Platform Cookbook*, both by Packt Publishing.

Packt is searching for authors like you

If you're interested in becoming an author for Packt, please visit `authors.packtpub.com` and apply today. We have worked with thousands of developers and tech professionals, just like you, to help them share their insight with the global tech community. You can make a general application, apply for a specific hot topic that we are recruiting an author for, or submit your own idea.

Table of Contents

Preface

Google Cloud Platform (GCP) is one of the fastest growing cloud technology providers in the market today. This book focuses on giving you an introduction to GCP and sets you on a path to becoming an expert as you learn more and delve deeper. Google has been a leader in implementing cutting-edge technologies within their data centers to bring user-friendly services to the masses. You will find that through GCP, Google has exposed these advanced technologies to the market. Now any application deployed in GCP can make use of these technologies, including containers, artificial intelligence, and machine learning.

This book hopes to give you a hands-on introduction to GCP. You will deploy virtual machines and containers using Kubernetes, and configure networking. This book also aims at giving you a high-level overview of the different products offered in GCP.

Who this book is for

Google Cloud Platform Administration is for administrators, cloud architects, and engineers who want to leverage the up-and-coming GCP. Some basic understanding of cloud computing will be useful.

What this book covers

Chapter 1, *Introduction to Google Cloud Platform*, introduces you to GCP with an overview of history and its concepts.

Chapter 2, *Google Cloud Platform Compute*, lets you explore and learn more about Google's Compute Engine platform, which is used to deploy virtual machines.

Chapter 3, *Google Cloud Platform Storage*, introduces you to the different storage offerings in GCP.

Chapter 4, *Google Cloud Platform Networking*, explores all the rich networking constructs you have available in GCP.

Chapter 5, *Google Cloud Platform Containers*, is a fun chapter where you will learn how to deploy containers using Kubernetes.

Chapter 6, *Google Cloud Platform Operations*, will teach you about the Stackdriver suite of products, which lets you manage and debug your applications.

Chapter 7, *Google Cloud Platform Identity and Security*, teaches you about Google's identity and security functionality for securing your GCP environment.

Chapter 8, *Google Cloud Platform Billing*, teaches you about the various aspects of billing, including analyzing bills and setting up budgets.

Chapter 9, *Google Cloud Platform Tools*, explores the tools available for deploying your application and also the rich marketplace that is available for you to deploy to.

To get the most out of this book

Before starting to read the book, some basic understanding of cloud computing would be useful. This book intends to launch your career with Google Cloud Platform. Continued and hands on learning is necessary to become an expert at GCP.

Download the color images

We also provide a PDF file that has color images of the screenshots/diagrams used in this book. You can download it here:
https://www.packtpub.com/sites/default/files/downloads/9781788624350_ColorImage
s.pdf.

Conventions used

There are a number of text conventions used throughout this book.

CodeInText: Indicates code words in text, database table names, folder names, filenames, file extensions, pathnames, dummy URLs, user input, and Twitter handles. Here is an example: "You can create an instance from an image using the Google Cloud Platform console, the gcloud command-line tool, or the API, by following these steps."

A block of code is set as follows:

```
    kind: PersistentVolumeClaim
apiVersion: v1
metadata:
    name: myvolumeclaim
spec:
```

Any command-line input or output is written as follows:

```
$ kubectl exec -it mywebapp-1-68fb69df68-4tcpp -- /bin/bash
```

Bold: Indicates a new term, an important word, or words that you see onscreen. For example, words in menus or dialog boxes appear in the text like this. Here is an example: "Open up your workload and click on **Expose**."

Warnings or important notes appear like this.

Tips and tricks appear like this.

Get in touch

Feedback from our readers is always welcome.

General feedback: If you have questions about any aspect of this book, mention the book title in the subject of your message and email us at customercare@packtpub.com.

Errata: Although we have taken every care to ensure the accuracy of our content, mistakes do happen. If you have found a mistake in this book, we would be grateful if you would report this to us. Please visit www.packt.com/submit-errata, selecting your book, clicking on the Errata Submission Form link, and entering the details.

Piracy: If you come across any illegal copies of our works in any form on the Internet, we would be grateful if you would provide us with the location address or website name. Please contact us at copyright@packt.com with a link to the material.

If you are interested in becoming an author: If there is a topic that you have expertise in and you are interested in either writing or contributing to a book, please visit authors.packtpub.com.

Reviews

Please leave a review. Once you have read and used this book, why not leave a review on the site that you purchased it from? Potential readers can then see and use your unbiased opinion to make purchase decisions, we at Packt can understand what you think about our products, and our authors can see your feedback on their book. Thank you!

For more information about Packt, please visit `packt.com`.

Introduction to Google Cloud Platform

1

This chapter begins with a brief introduction to cloud computing. We then introduce the **Google Cloud Platform** (**GCP**) with an overview of its history and its concepts. We will then look into some of its concepts, tools, and services. We will also map and compare how **Amazon Web Services** (**AWS**) and Microsoft Azure public clouds match up to GCP products. Lastly, we will set up an account in GCP using the free tier that allows you a 12-month, $300 free trial of all GCP products.

In this chapter, we will cover the following:

- Introduction to cloud computing
- Introduction to GCP
- GCP services
- Data centers and regions
- AWS and Azure in comparison to GCP
- Exploring GCP

Introduction to cloud computing

In the simplest terms, cloud computing is the practice of delivering computing services such as servers, storage, networking, databases, and applications over the internet. In such a delivery model, the consumer, typically a business or an enterprise, only pays for the resources they use without having to pay for the capital investment cost of building and maintaining the data centers.

There are both financial and technological benefits for adopting a cloud computing approach. Companies transform their capital costs to operational costs and are able to pay for what they use rather than pay for idle infrastructure. Cloud computing also eliminates the cost of purchasing and maintaining expensive hardware and data center space. The **pay-as-you-go** model allows for increasing or decreasing resource consumption without having to pre-purchase hardware.

Companies can also focus on rapid innovation without having to worry about the backend infrastructure's ability to support it. Cloud companies are rapidly introducing new services on high performance hardware platforms that can be consumed on-demand by end users. Typically, companies either migrate entirely to the cloud or use a hybrid model of connecting their on-premise infrastructure to a cloud provider and migrate workloads as needed.

Some good initial use cases for the cloud include development and testing environments, data archiving, data mining, and disaster recovery. All these cases will help reduce capital costs and the speed of deployment and consumption makes cloud computing an ideal platform for these use cases.

Most cloud computing services fall into three broad categories: **Infrastructure as a Service (IaaS)**, **Platform as a Service (PaaS)**, and **Software as a Service (SaaS)**.

With IaaS, you rent the IT infrastructure, which includes servers, virtual machines, networks, storage, and operating systems, on a pay-as-you-go basis. With PaaS, you are given access to an on-demand environment that allows you to quickly deploy, test, and develop your application without having to worry about the underlying IT infrastructure. PaaS is ideal for developers who only care about quickly deploying their application and not worrying about the server, compute, or its storage.

SaaS is a way of delivering software applications over the internet on a subscription model. A good example of SaaS is your Gmail email account. You are subscribed to your email by signing up for it and use the **email software** that is written, maintained, secured, and managed by Google.

Introducing GCP

GCP's initial release was on October 6, 2011. Since then it has become one of the most used public cloud platforms and is continuing to grow. GCP offers a suite of cloud services that run on the same infrastructure that Google uses to host their end-user products such as Google search, Gmail, and YouTube. This makes it important because Google not only continues to innovate for its customers but also benefits from its own investment into the platform. Google began operations by launching its Google App engine back in 2008. Since then we have seen multiple other services introduced and the list keeps on growing.

GCP services

While GCP services are many, we can broadly categorize them into four different services. They are compute services, storage services, networking services, and big data services. Apart from these, there are other cloud services such as identity and security management, management tools, data transfer, and machine learning.

Compute services

GCP offers you a wide variety of computing services that allow you complete flexibility as to how you want to manage your computing assets. Depending on your application and its requirements, you can choose to deploy a traditional custom virtual machine or use Google's App Engine to run the application:

- **Compute engine**: Allows you to deploy and run high-performance virtual machines in Google data centers. You can deploy either a pre-configured virtual machine or customize the resources as per your requirements.
- **Apps engine**: Allows you to deploy your application on a fully managed platform which is completely supported by Google. This allows you to simply deploy your application and have it running without you having to worry about the underlying infrastructure.

- **Kubernetes engine**: This service allows you to run containers on GCP. This means your containerized applications can be deployed on GCP using the Kubernetes engine service without you having to manage the underlying cluster yourself. **Google's Site Reliability Engineers** (**SREs**) constantly monitor the cluster, which relieves you of that responsibility.
- **Cloud Functions**: This service allows you to run code and respond to events on the fly in a true serverless model. This means allowing code to respond to events is determined by you. This also means you will be billed only if your code runs, making it very cost effective.

Storage services

The following are the types of storage services:

- **Cloud storage:** An object storage that can be used for a variety of use cases and is accessible via a REST API. This offering allows geo-redundancy with its multi-regional capability and can be used for both high performance storage requirements to archival storage.
- **Cloud SQL:** A fully managed (replicated and backed-up) database service that allows you to easily get started with your MySQL and PostgreSQL databases in the cloud. The offering also comes with a standard API and also built-in migration tools to migrate your current databases to the cloud.
- **Cloud BigTable**: Cloud BigTable is the database for all your NoSQL database requirements. The service can scale to hundreds of petabytes easily, which makes it suitable for enterprise data analysis. BigTable also integrates easily with other big data tools such as Hadoop.
- **Cloud Spanner**: Cloud Spanner is a relational database service that aims at providing highly scalable and strongly consistent database service for the cloud. This is a fully managed service that can offer transactional consistency and synchronous replication of databases across multiple geographies.
- **Cloud Datastore**: Cloud Datastore is another service set apart from Cloud BigTable that is suitable for your key-value pair NoSQL database requirements. The services comes with other features such as sharding and replication.
- **Persistent Disk**: Persistent Disk is persistent high performance block storage that can be attached to your Google compute engine instance or Google Kubernetes engine. The service allows you to resize storage without any downtime and is offered in both HDD and SSD formats. You can also mount one disk on multiple machine instances allowing multi-reader capability.

Networking services

These are the networking services:

- **Virtual Private Cloud** (**VPC**): Virtual private cloud allows you to connect multiple GCP resources together or create internal isolated resources that can be managed easily. You can also deploy firewalls, **Virtual Private Networks** (**VPNs**), routes, and custom IP ranges.
- **Cloud load balancing**: This service allows you to distribute your incoming traffic across multiple Google Compute Engines. Cloud load balancing also lets you do autoscaling and can scale your backend instances depending on the incoming traffic load.
- **Cloud CDN**: Google's cloud delivery network allows you to distribute your content for lower latency and faster access. Google has over 90 edge points globally spread across multiple continents that make it easy for you to decrease your serving costs.
- **Cloud interconnect**: This service allows you to directly connect your on-premises data center to Google's network. You can either peer with Google or interconnect depending on your bandwidth requirements and peering capabilities.
- **Cloud DNS**: This is Google's highly available global DNS network and comes with an API to allow management of records and zones.

Big data

The following are the big data services:

- **BigQuery**: BigQuery is an enterprise data warehouse that allows you to store and query massive datasets by enabling fast SQL queries using Google's underlying infrastructure.
- **Cloud dataflow**: A fully managed service that allows real-time batch and stream data processing. The service also integrates with Stackdriver, Google's unified logging and monitoring solution, letting you monitor and troubleshoot issues as they happen.
- **Cloud dataproc**: Cloud dataproc is a fully managed cloud service to run Apache spark and Apache Hadoop clusters.

- **Cloud datalab**: A powerful tool that allows you to explore and visualize large datasets.
- **Cloud dataprep**: A service that helps in structured and unstructured data analysis by means of visually exploring and cleaning it.
- **Cloud pub/sub**: A service built for stream analytics that allows you to publish and subscribe to data streams for big data analysis.
- **Google genomics**: A service that allows you to query the genomic information of large research projects.
- **Google DataStudio**: Allows you to turn your data into informative dashboards.

We will look at all services in greater detail in the following chapters.

Data centers and regions

GCP services are located across North and South America, Europe, Asia, and Australia. These locations are further divided into regions and zones. A region is an independent geographic area that consists of one or more zones. In total, Google has about 17 regions, 52 zones, and over 100 points of presence (points of presence is a local access point for an ISP). Each zone is identified by a letter, for example, zone **a** in the US-Central region is named `us-central1-a`.

When you deploy a cloud resource, they get deployed in a specific region and in a specific zone within that region. Any resource deployed in a single zone will not be redundant—if the zone fails, so will the resource. If you need fault tolerance and high availability, you must deploy the resource in multiple zones within that region to protect against unexpected failures. A disaster recovery plan will be needed in order to protect your entire application against a regional failure.

All regions are expected to have a minimum of three zones:

Region	Zones	Location
asia-east1	a, b, c	Changhua County, Taiwan
asia-northeast1	a, b, c	Tokyo, Japan
asia-south1	a, b, c	Mumbai, India
asia-southeast1	a, b, c	Jurong West, Singapore
australia-southeast1	a, b, c	Sydney, Australia
europe-north1	a, b, c	Hamina, Finland
europe-west1	b, c, d	St. Ghislain, Belgium
europe-west2	a, b, c	London, England, UK
europe-west3	a, b, c	Frankfurt, Germany
europe-west4	a, b, c	Eemshaven, Netherlands
northamerica-northeast1	a, b, c	Montréal, Québec, Canada
southamerica-east1	a, b, c	São Paulo, Brazil
us-central1	a, b, c, f	Council Bluffs, Iowa, USA
us-east1	b, c, d	Moncks Corner, South Carolina, USA
us-east4	a, b, c	Ashburn, Northern Virginia, USA
us-west1	a, b, c	The Dalles, Oregon, USA
us-west2	a, b, c	Los Angeles, California, USA

 Note that not all regions and zones provide all GCP services. For example, the Oregon region has three regions within it and does not offer Google App Engine services. So it is critical to understand your application requirements and place it in the appropriate region that supports it.

The roundtrip latency of networks between zones within a region is less than 5 ms:

Current regions and number of zones	Oregon, Los Angeles, Iowa, South Carolina, North Virginia, Montreal, Sao Paolo, Netherlands, London, Belgium, Frankfurt, Mumbai, Finland, Singapore, Sydney, Taiwan, Tokyo
Future regions and number of zones	Hong Kong, Osaka, Zurich

Relating AWS and Azure to GCP

If you are familiar with Amazon's AWS or Microsoft's Azure, then this table will help you relate their associated services to what GCP has to offer. Only a few services are shown in the table:

Amazon Web Services	Microsoft Azure	Google Cloud Platform
Amazon EC2	Azure Virtual Machines	Google Compute Engine
AWS Elastic Beanstalk	Azure App Services	Google App Engine
Amazon EC2 Container Service	Azure Container Service	Google Kubernetes Engine
Amazon DynamoDB	Azure Cosmos DB	Google Cloud Bigtable
Amazon Redshift	Microsoft Azure SQL Data warehouse	Google BigQuery
Amazon Lambda	Azure Functions	Google Cloud Functions
Amazon S3	Azure Blob Storage	Google Storage
AWS Direct Connect	Azure ExpressRoute	Google Cloud Interconnect
AWS SNS	Azure Service Bus	Google Cloud Pub/Sub
AWS Cloudwatch	Application Insights	Stackdriver Monitoring

Exploring GCP

Let's dive a little deeper into GCP by creating an account and getting familiar with the console and command-line interface. There are three ways to access GCP—via console, via a command-line interface using the gcloud command-line tool, and Google Cloud SDK client libraries. But before that, we need to understand the concept of projects.

In GCP, all resources must belong to a project. If you work for a large organization, don't be surprised to see tens of hundreds of projects. Projects can be tied down to a business unit or an internal or external organization.

In GCP, any cloud resources that you create must belong to a project. A project is basically an organizing entity for any cloud resource that you wish to deploy. All resources deployed within a single project can communicate easily with each other, for example two compute engine virtual machines can easily communicate with each other within a project without having to go through a gateway. This, however, is subject to region and zone limitations. It is important to note that resources in one project can talk to resources in another project only through an external network connection.

Each project has a project name, a project ID, and a project number. The project ID has to be a unique name across the cloud platform (or Google can generate an ID for you). Remember that even if the project has been deleted, its ID cannot be reused again:

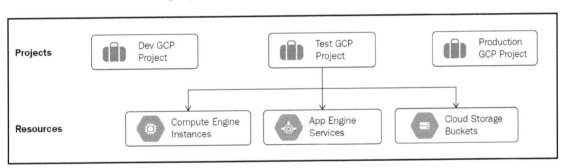

GCP allows you a free trail that provides you with $300 of credit towards any Google product. Your trial lasts for 12 months and expires automatically after that. If you exceed your free $300 credit, your services will be turned off but you will not be charged or billed, making this a safe way to explore and learn more about GCP.

To get started:

1. Go to `https://cloud.google.com` and click on **TRY IT FREE**:

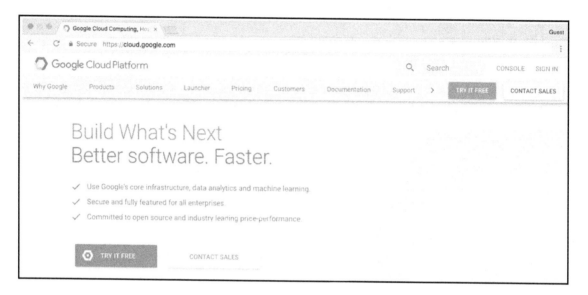

 Remember that you will need to have a Google registered ID to be able to register to use GCP services. We will discuss accounts and access in greater detail in cloud identity and access management.

2. Once you create an account and log in, agree to the terms and conditions and fill out your details along with a valid credit card number.

3. Once logged in you will see a **Billing Overview**:

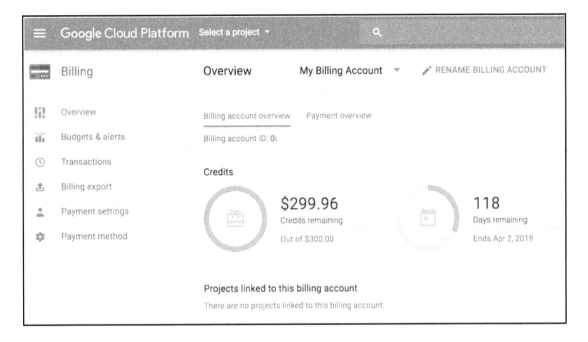

Let's look at how to access different GCP services using the console:

1. Click on the menu on the left to drop down the list of services. Feel free to scroll down this list to explore:

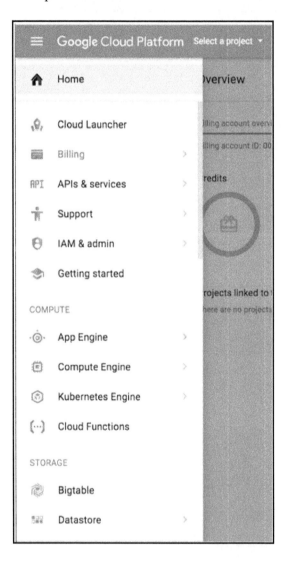

2. On the right, let's look at another way of accessing your GCP instance using the cloud shell tool that allows you to manage your resources from the command line in any browser. The [>_] on the top right activates your Google cloud shell. This opens a new frame at the bottom of the browser and displays a prompt. It may take a few seconds for the shell session to be established:

Creating your first project

Alternatively, if you prefer using your terminal, you can download and install the SDK to use gcloud on your terminal. It is important to remember that gcloud is part of the Google Cloud SDK.

We can get started at deploying services by first creating a project:

1. In the preceding illustration, click **Create** to create your first project:

2. You can pick any project name and GCP auto-generates a project ID for you. If you need to customize the project ID in accordance with your organization's standards, click **Edit**. Remember that this project ID needs to be unique.
3. Click **Create** when done.

4. Once the project is created, your **DASHBOARD** will show you all info related to your project and its associated resources:

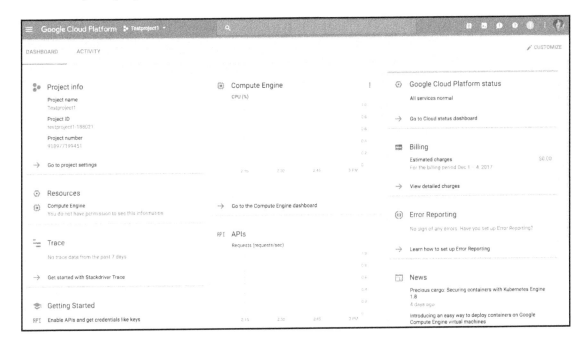

Project IDs are auto-generated but can be customized. It is best to leave the default project IDs in place to avoid management issues.

5. On the left, note the **Project name, Project ID**, and the **Project number**.

6. Click on **Project settings**. You will see that you are able to change the **Project name** but cannot change the **Project ID** or the **Project number**. Project settings can also be accessed by going to **IAM & admin | Settings**:

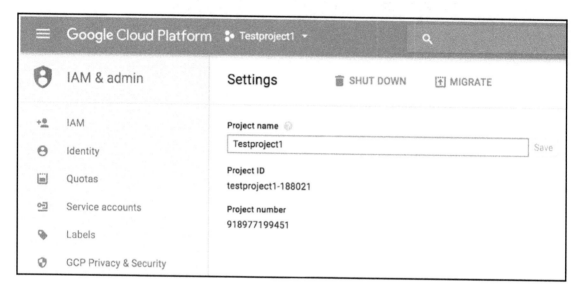

You can even shut down a project by clicking on the **Shut Down** option. This will cause all traffic and billing to stop on the project and shut down all resources within a project. You will have 30 days to restore such a project before its deleted. You also have an option to migrate a project. This comes in handy if you are part of an organization and want to move a project over to the organization unit. You will be able to do this if you are a G suite or a cloud premium customer with a support package. Ideally, this is something that keeps projects and permissions at an organization level, rather than at an individual level.

Let's look at enabling APIs as services for your project to allow us to use API access to services. APIs are automatically enabled whenever you try to launch a service using the console. For example, if you attempt to deploy a Google Compute Engine virtual machine, the initialization of that service will enable the Google Cloud Compute API:

1. Go to **Menu | API's and Services | Dashboard**:

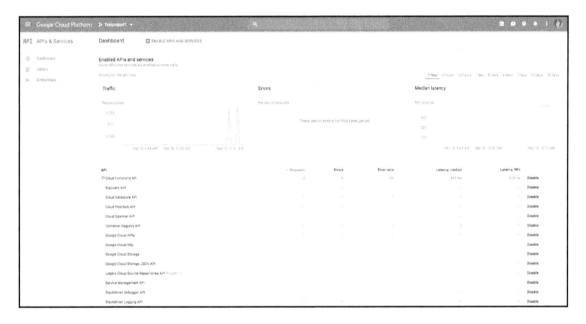

All APIs associated with services are disabled by default and you can enable specific ones as required by your application.

2. Click on **ENABLE APIS AND SERVICES** and search for the `Google Cloud Compute API`. Click **Enable**. You can also click on **Try this API** to test the API through the browser console.

Once the API is enabled, you will see all the info related to this API in the dashboard. You can even choose to disable the API if needed:

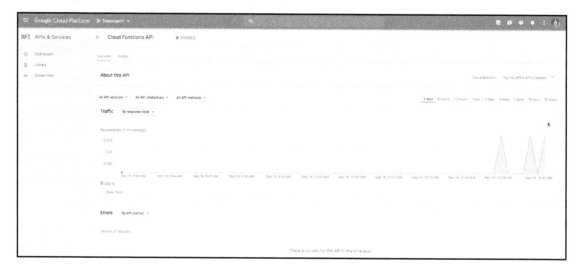

API in the dashboard

Using the command line

Let's look at using the gcloud command to create a project. gcloud is part of the Google Cloud SDK. You will need to download and install it on your machine in order to use the gcloud commands from your terminal. Alternatively, you may use the cloud shell console from within the browser. Go to `https://cloud.google.com/sdk/downloads` to download the relevant package as it applies to your machine and install it:

1. Once you have installed the SDK on your machine, we need to initialize it. This is done by running the `gcloud init` command to perform the initial setup tasks. If you ever need to change a setting or create a new configuration, simply re-run `gcloud init`.

2. Open the terminal on your machine and type `gcloud init`. This opens a browser to allow you to log in to your account. If you want to avoid the browser, type `gcloud init --console-only`.

3. If you use the `-console-only flag`, then copy and paste the browser URL in the terminal and then copy the key back into the console:

4. Enter the numeric choice for the project to use. To create new project, type 2:

```
You are logged in as: [singh.ranjit@gmail.com].

Pick cloud project to use:
 [1] testproject1-188021
 [2] Create a new project
Please enter numeric choice or text value (must exactly match list
item):  2

Enter a Project ID. Note that a Project ID CANNOT be changed later.
Project IDs must be 6-30 characters (lowercase ASCII, digits, or
hyphens) in length and start with a lowercase letter. 
```

5. Enter a unique project ID and click *Enter*. This will create a new project.
6. To list all projects, type `gcloud projects list`:

```
[usenthakur6m1:~ thakur6$ gcloud projects list
PROJECT_ID              NAME                    PROJECT_NUMBER
testproject1-188021     Testproject1            918977199451
testproject2-998189     testproject2-998189     1077246767336
usenthakur6m1:~ thakur6$
```

Summary

We are off to a good start with a brief understanding of the history of GCP and its services. We looked at all the data center regions where GCP is offered and discussed their aspects and also a list of services. We also spent time creating a free tier account and explored the GCP console and created projects.

In `Chapter 2`, *Google Cloud Platform Compute*, we will look into learning about GCP Compute and its various aspects.

2
Google Cloud Platform Compute

In this chapter, we will look at the **Google Cloud Platform** (**GCP**) compute services. Google Compute Engine, Google App Engine, Google Container Engine, and Google Cloud Functions are the four key services that make up the GCP compute offering. For each of these services, we will look at their basic options and go over their basic deployment.

In this chapter, we will cover:

- Google Compute Engine
- Google App Engine
- Kubernetes engine
- Google Cloud Functions

Google Compute Engine

The Google Compute Engine service lets you create and run virtual machine instances on GCP. Just like any other cloud provider, Google lets you deploy and manage virtual machine instances in a true **Infrastructure as a Service** (**IaaS**) fashion. Google Compute Engine also supports a variety of operating systems including Windows Server 2008 R2, 2012 R2 and 2016, Red Hat, Ubuntu, SUSE, CentOS, CoreOS, and Debian. You can even import a disk image from your on-premises environment. Each instance is part of a project and contains a small persistent root disk and more storage can be added depending on your requirements. A **virtual private cloud** (**VPC**) network can also be attached to an instance with an assigned IP address. We will discuss storage and networking requirements more later in this chapter.

VPC is a networking construct that allows you to isolate your cloud services.

GCP offers predefined machine types that fit the needs of different applications. You can also define your own custom machine type as well. Predefined machine types are classified into three different classes: standard machine type, high memory machine type, and high CPU machine type.

Standard machine types of machines are most suitable for day-to-day applications that are not memory or CPU intensive. Standard machine types allocate 3.75 GB of RAM per virtual CPU. On an n1 series machine, a virtual CPU is implemented as a single hardware hyper-thread on a variety of Intel CPUs ranging from Sandy Bridge to Skylake:

Machine name	Virtual CPUs	Memory (GB)	Max number of persistent disks (PD)	Max total PD size (TB)
n1-standard-1	1	3.75	16 (32 in Beta)	64
n1-standard-2	2	7.50	16 (64 in Beta)	64
n1-standard-4	4	15	16 (64 in Beta)	64
n1-standard-8	8	30	16 (128 in Beta)	64
n1-standard-16	16	60	16 (128 in Beta)	64
n1-standard-32	32	120	16 (128 in Beta)	64
n1-standard-64	64	240	16 (128 in Beta)	64
n1-standard-96 (Beta)	96	360	16 (128 in Beta)	64

For applications requiring more memory than CPU, high memory machine types are ideal. These virtual machines have double the amount of RAM (6.50 GB) per CPU than that of standard machine types:

Machine name	Virtual CPUs	Memory (GB)	Max number of persistent disks (PD)	Max total PD size
n1-highmem-2	2	13	16 (64 in Beta)	64
n1-highmem-4	4	26	16 (64 in Beta)	64
n1-highmem-8	8	52	16 (128 in Beta)	64
n1-highmem-16	16	104	16 (128 in Beta)	64
n1-highmem-32	32	208	16 (128 in Beta)	64
n1-highmem-64	64	416	16 (128 in Beta)	64
n1-highmem-96 (Beta)	96	624	16 (128 in Beta)	64

High CPU machine types are for applications requiring high CPU over memory. These machine types have 0.9 GB of RAM per virtual CPU:

Machine name	Virtual CPUs	Memory (GB)	Max number of persistent disks (PD)	Max total PD size (TB)
n1-highcpu-2	2	1.80	16 (64 in Beta)	64
n1-highcpu-4	4	3.60	16 (64 in Beta)	64
n1-highcpu-8	8	7.20	16 (128 in Beta)	64
n1-highcpu-16	16	14.4	16 (128 in Beta)	64
n1-highcpu-32	32	28.8	16 (128 in Beta)	64
n1-highcpu-64	64	57.6	16 (128 in Beta)	64
n1-highcpu-96 (Beta)	96	86.4	16 (128 in Beta)	64

f1-micro bursting machine types

f1-micro bursting machine types allow instances to use additional physical CPU for short periods of time. If your instance requires more CPU than originally allocated, it can take advantage of the additional physical CPU instance. Burst instances are temporary and are only possible periodically:

Machine name	Virtual CPUs	Memory (GB)	Max number of persistent disks (PD)	Max total PD size (TB)
f1-micro	0.2	0.60	4 (16 in Beta)	3
g1-small	0.5	1.70	4 (16 in Beta)	3

Mega-memory machine types

Mega-memory machine types are for those applications that require higher memory to virtual CPU ratios. This is different from the high memory machine type where higher memory is offered without high virtual CPUs. Mega-memory machine types offer 15 GB of RAM per virtual CPU. Not all regions offer mega-memory machine types:

Machine name	Virtual CPUs	Memory (GB)	Max number of persistent disks (PD)	Max total PD size (TB)
n1-megamem-96	96	1433.6	16 (128 in Beta)	64
n1-ultramem-40	40	961	16 (128 in Beta)	64
n1-ultramem-80	80	1922	16 (128 in Beta)	64
n1-ultramem-160	160	3844	16 (128 in Beta)	64

Images

A compute engine allows you to deploy operating systems using either public images or custom images. Public images are maintained by Google, third-party vendors, and open source communities. All projects have access to these images to create instances. Custom images can be created in your project and are available only to your project. You can even import a custom image from your data center into GCP at no cost other than the image storage charge.

All public images are 64-bit versions of the operating systems. Only some of the public images are supported by the compute engine team:

Operating system	Supported by	Image family	Image project	Notes
CentOS	Compute engine	`centos-7` `centos-6`	`centos-cloud`	

Container-optimized OS from Google	Compute engine	`cos-stable`
		`cos-beta`
		`cos-dev`
			`cos-cloud`	

CoreOS	CoreOS support	`coreos-stable`
		`coreos-beta`
		`coreos-alpha`
			`coreos-cloud`	

Debian	Compute engine	`debian-9` `debian-8`	`debian-cloud`	
Red Hat Enterprise Linux (RHEL)	Compute engine	`rhel-7` `rhel-6`	`rhel-cloud`	Premium image additional cost
SUSE Enterprise Linux Server (SLES)	Compute engine	`sles-12` `sles-11`	`suse-cloud`	Premium image additional cost
SLES for SAP	Compute engine	`sles-12-sp2-sap` `sles-12-sp1-sap`	`suse-sap-cloud`	Premium image additional cost

Ubuntu	Compute engine	`ubuntu-1604-lts`
		`ubuntu-1404-lts`
		`ubuntu-1710`
			`ubuntu-os-cloud`	

Windows server	Compute engine	`windows-1709-core`
		`windows-1709-core-for-containers`
		`windows-2016`
		`windows-2016-core`
		`windows-2012-r2`
		`windows-2012-r2-core`
		`windows-2008-r2`
			`windows-cloud`	Premium image additional cost

SQL server on Windows server	Compute engine	`SQL Server image families`	`windows-sql-cloud`	Premium image

Creating a VM instance

Let's look at deploying a virtual machine instance using an machine image. Once the image is deployed, the compute engine automatically starts the instance. The following diagram describes the high-level process of how a machine image can be used to deploy a compute instance. The image archive, which consists of the master boot records and the relevant partitions, is uploaded to cloud storage. You can then create a template/image, persistent disks, and then create a compute instance to boot off these disks:

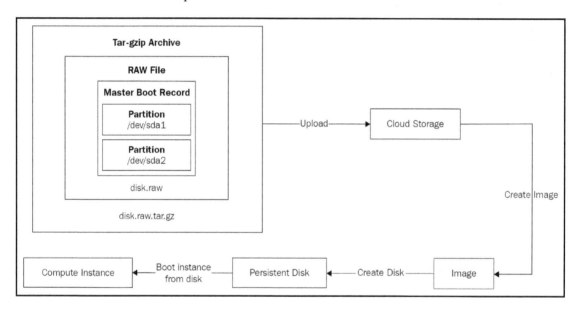

You can create an instance from an image using the Google Cloud Platform console, the `gcloud` command-line tool or the API by following these steps:

1. Log in to your Google Cloud Platform console, select a project and click on **VM Instances**.

Remember to have the right permissions set on your account to allow you to create instances.

2. Click on the **CREATE INSTANCE** button.

In production, remember to have generic friendly names for your resources and instances. These names are displayed in support and operational dashboards in GCP and masking their names will help enhance security.

2. Enter an instance name and select a zone where the instance will be deployed. You will also see the cost of deploying the instance on the right.

3. You can click on the machine type or customize it to create a custom machine type with your desired CPU and memory.

4. Depending on the zone, you will be able to deploy GPUs.

5. Select a boot disk to deploy the image from. Click on **Change** if you want to pick another operating system image to deploy. You also get to set a size for your persistent boot disk and can pick between disk types. We will discuss storage disks further in this chapter.

6. You can create labels, set disk behavior upon instance deletion, add additional disks, and pick network interfaces. We will discuss network interfaces in further chapters.

7. Click **Create** when done. You will see the instance created, as shown in the following screenshot:

9. You can **Start**, **Stop**, and manage the instance as shown:

10. To get more details about the instance, click on the instance name. We will look into monitoring and utilization in greater detail in upcoming chapters:

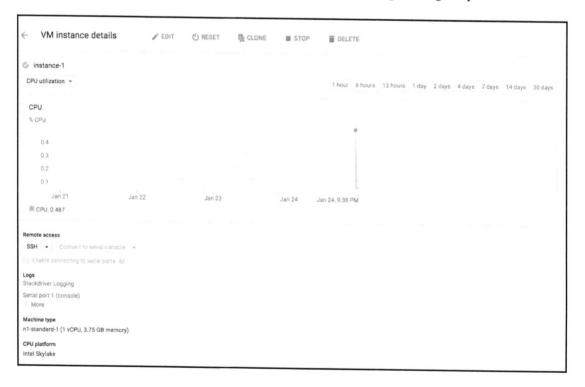

Did you know that you can enable interactive access to an instance's serial console so you can connect and troubleshoot instances. You can find more information here—`https://cloud.google.com/compute/docs/instances/interacting-with-serial-console`.

Preemptible VM instances

Preemptible instances are VM instances that can be created at a much lower price than a regular instance. The only difference is that the compute engine can terminate these instances if those resources need to be reclaimed for other tasks. Preemptible instances also have a 24-hour limit after which they are terminated.

If GCP determines that their data center load is increasing, they can, selectively, terminate your pre emptive VM instance, which can cause application disruption. It is very important that premptible instances be used only for applications that are fault-tolerant or batch-processing jobs.

Due to the limitations of preemptible instances, preemptible instances are not covered by any service level agreement.

Preemptible instances are created during VM instance creation. Just set the **Preemptibility** option to **On** to change the instance to a preemptible instance:

Availability policy

Preemptibility
A preemptible VM costs much less, but lasts only 24 hours. It can be terminated sooner due to system demands. Learn more

Off (recommended)

On

Compute Engine can automatically restart VM instances if they are terminated for non-

---

Live migration

A compute engine virtual machine instance can live migrate when a host system event occurs such as a software or a hardware update. This feature prevents unnecessary reboots of a virtual machine and can live migrate the virtual machine in the same zone. It is important to remember that live migration does not change the virtual machine configuration, but rather moves it to another host without any interruption.

It is important to remember that instances with GPUs cannot be live migrated. These virtual machines will need to be terminated. The compute engine provides a 60-minute notice before the virtual machine with the GPU is terminated. Preemptible instances cannot be live migrated either.

Instance templates

Instance templates are a way to save a virtual machine instance configuration so it can be deployed over and over again without having to set the configuration every single time. It is important to remember that creating a virtual machine using an instance template can only be done using the GCP API. You can create the instance templates using the GCP web portal.

The instance template is also not bound to a zone or a region and is a global resource. You also cannot change or update the configuration of an instance template. The only way to do this is to create a new instance template.

To create an instance template:

1. Click on **Instance templates** in the menu.
2. The process is similar to a VM instance creation. Once the desired configuration is set, click **Create**:

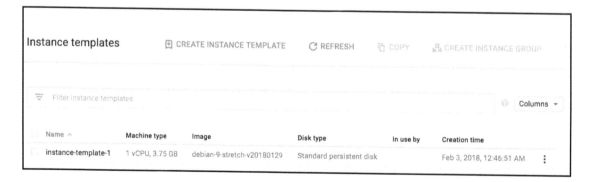

Google App Engine

Google App Engine is a **Platform as a Service** (**PaaS**) offering that allows you to quickly deploy your applications. The app engine environment automatically scales your app up or down depending on the load. You can also customize the runtime and the operating system of your app engine using Docker files.

App engine offers two different environments, the flexible environment and the standard environment. Depending on your use case, you can choose to use both environments simultaneously for your application.

The following table summarizes the differences between the two environments:

Feature	Flexible environment	Standard environment
Instance startup time	Minutes	Seconds
Maximum request timeout	60 minutes	60 seconds
Background threads	Yes	Yes, with restrictions
Background processes	Yes	No
SSH debugging	Yes	No
Scaling	Manual and automatic	Manual, basic, and automatic
Writing to local disk	Yes, ephemeral (disk initialized on each VM startup)	No
Modifying the runtime	Yes (through Dockerfile)	No
Automatic in-place security patches	Yes (excludes container image runtime)	Yes
Network access	Yes	Only via App Engine services (includes outbound sockets), and only for billing-enabled Python, Go, and PHP applications.
Supports installing third-party binaries	Yes	No
Location	North America, Asia Pacific, or Europe	North America, Asia Pacific, or Europe
Pricing	Based on usage of vCPU, memory, and persistent disks	Based on instance hours

Table 2.1: courtesy of Google

Before you start using the app engine, you need to download and install the SDK for the app engine. The process differs in the app engine environment and also depending on the development platform you choose. For more specific information on installing the SDK, refer to the app engine documentation link: `https://cloud.google.com/appengine/downloads`.

All the infrastructure that is required to run your app engine instance is located in one region and is redundantly available across all zones in a region. Ideally, you would want to deploy your app in a region that is close to your primary customer base. Once the app region is set, you cannot change it. The app engine is available in `northamerica-northeast1`, `us-central1`, `us-east1`, `us-east4`, `southamerica-east1`, `Europe-west1`, `Europe-west2`, `Europe-west3`, `asia-northeast1`, `asia-south1`, and `Australia-southeast1`.

Let's have a look at accessing the app engine from the Google Cloud Platform web UI.

Click on the top-level menu and click on **App Engine**:

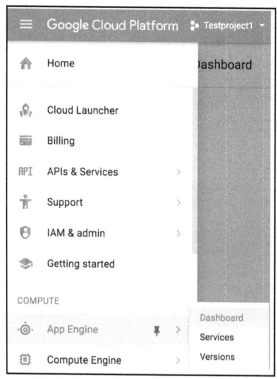

You can learn to deploy a new app with a guided deployment:

An interesting feature of the Google App Engine is its ability to deploy apps as a set of microservices that makes your app components independent and modular.

Kubernetes engine

One of the most interesting and sought-after features of Google cloud platform is its Kubernetes engine. The Google Kubernetes engine provides a way to deploy, manage, and scale your containerized applications. Kubernetes provides an environment that contains multiple compute engine instances that work together as a container cluster. Kubernetes engine gives you all the benefits of running clusters such as load balancing and automatic scaling and upgrades.

Kubernetes is a hot topic and is one of the most sought after skill in the market. Learning Kubernetes the GCP way is a valuable skill.

In Kubernetes, a container cluster consists of one or more cluster master and multiple machine instances called nodes. These machine instances are compute engine instances that work as a cluster node. All your containers run on top of this container cluster. You can create multiple container clusters to run different containerized applications as needed:

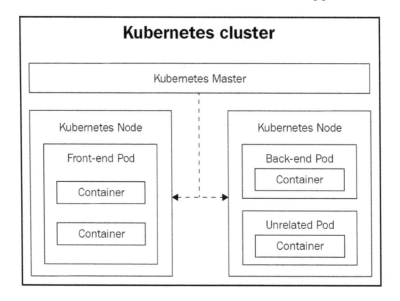

All the control plane processes are run and handled by the cluster master. This includes the Kubernetes API server, scheduler, and the core resource controllers. The Kubernetes engine manages the cluster master including the upgrades to the Kubernetes version running on the cluster master. The cluster master's API acts as a hub for all communication to the cluster. All internal processes act as clients of the API server, which makes the API server a **single source of truth** for the entire cluster.

 Upgrades can be set to automatic or manual depending on your preference.

The cluster master is responsible for scheduling workloads on each of the cluster's nodes. The cluster master schedules workloads (containerized applications) and manages their life cycle, scaling, and upgrades.

Let's look at how a Kubernetes cluster is deployed using the Kubernetes engine:

1. Log in to your GCP portal and click on the top menu. Make sure a project is selected.

2. Click on **Kubernetes Engine**:

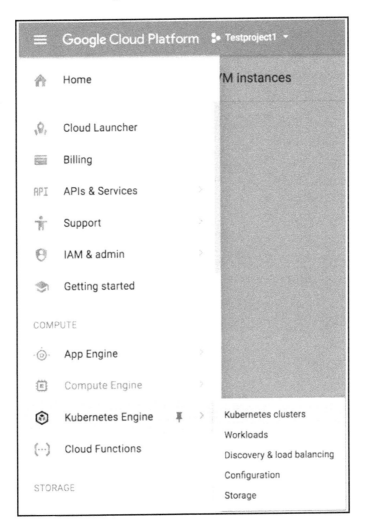

If this is the first time deploying Kubernetes, GCP takes a few minutes to initialize the service.

3. Select **Kubernetes clusters** and click **Create Cluster**:

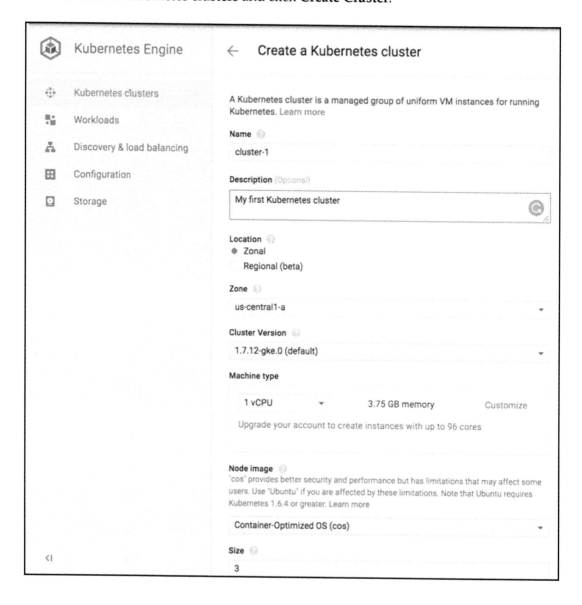

4. Enter a **Name** for the cluster and a **Description**. Clusters can be either **Zonal** or **Regional (beta)**. A zonal cluster allows you to deploy nodes in multiple zones in a region. In such a deployment, you will have one cluster master managing nodes in multiple zones. In a regional cluster, you can have one or more cluster master managing nodes in multiple regions.

Cluster Version here shows you the version of Kubernetes that will get deployed on the cluster master. You can choose a different version if you like:

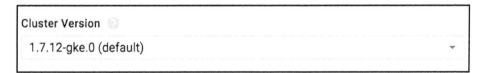

Google offers two supported node images that are deployed on your compute engine—nodes that are part of this Kubernetes cluster. You can either pick from a **Container-Optimized OS (cos)** which is maintained and managed by Google, or **Ubuntu**:

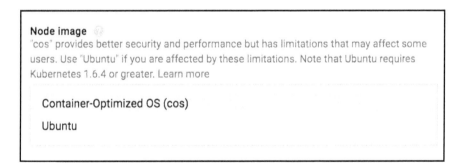

Next select the **Size** of this cluster. Entering 3 here causes the cluster to deploy three nodes (compute engine instances). You will be billed for three nodes. These three nodes will be deployed with the specifications you picked in the machine type. You will see the total cores and the total memory for the three nodes combined. Also take note that the cluster instances (nodes) use ephemeral local disks, meaning if the node is lost, then so is the data on the disk. If you need persistent disks attached to your containers, you will need to add them:

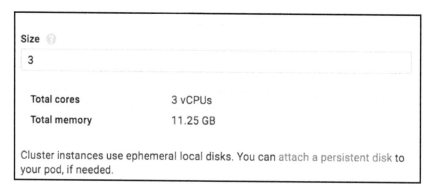

Automatic node upgrades allow you to automatically upgrade the Kubernetes version whenever an upgrade is available. You can **Enable** or **Disable** this option during deployment or at a later time:

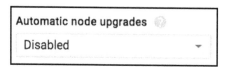

The **Automatic node repair (beta)** feature helps you to keep the nodes in the cluster in a functional state. The Kubernetes engine makes periodic checks on the health state of each of the cluster nodes. If the Kubernetes engine detects a node failure, it initiates repair processes that involve recreating the node:

Stackdriver Logging and **Stackdriver Monitoring** allow you to capture all the logs and monitor the cluster performance:

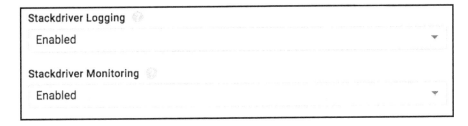

Under the **Advanced** options, you can select and opt for more customizations including additional zones, autoscaling, preemptible nodes, and even boot disk size. In addition to these, you can define custom networks, select **SSD disks**, and select a **Maintenance window (beta)**.

5. Click **Create** to create your cluster:

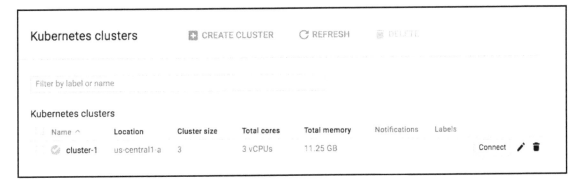

You will see your cluster along with three nodes deployed in the compute engine:

Each node is managed by the cluster master (cluster-1 in this preceding example) and receives updates as needed. Each of these nodes runs the necessary services to support Docker containers that make up the cluster **workloads**. A workload includes the Docker runtime and the Kubernetes node agent (kubelet), which communicates with the master and is responsible for starting and running Docker containers within that node. To run these services (and some other services/agents, which include log collection and intra-cluster network connectivity), some CPU and memory is consumed from the nodes. The resources consumed are minimal but need to be considered when deciding upon the resources needed for your containers.

 At this time, the Kubernetes engine only supports Docker containers on the nodes.

Node pools

Within a cluster, you can create pools of nodes that are identical to each other. When you create a cluster, the number and type of nodes you specify becomes the default-node-pool. You can add more nodes to this pool or create a different set of node pools that is managed by the same cluster. Creating additional node pools comes in handy when you have a containerized application with a different set of resource requirements.

To create a node pool:

1. Click on the **Kubernetes cluster** and click on **EDIT** and scroll to the bottom to find **Node Pools**:

2. Here you can either change the **Size** of the current node pool, the `default-pool`, delete it, or click on **Add node pool**. This opens up a fresh set of options to add to your additional node pool:

3. Click **Save** to deploy the second node pool. This deploys two more nodes in the compute engine that are part of the pool and are managed by the same cluster:

Kubernetes and workload deployment are deep concepts and deserve their own book. Kubernetes is a very powerful tool if used appropriately for your applications. Refer to the official Google Kubernetes engine documentation and learn more at `https://Kubernetes.io`.

Google Cloud Functions

Google Cloud Functions is a serverless environment for building and connecting cloud services. Developers and users write simple-purpose functions that are executed in response to an event that may be generated from your cloud instances or infrastructure. When the event being watched is triggered, the cloud function executes in a fully managed environment. This kind of approach saves a lot of time because a developer need not worry about having to deploy the underlying infrastructure that is required to run their code. Cloud functions remove the additional overhead of managing the environment and give a developer a fully managed execution environment that can readily be used.

Cloud functions are written in JavaScript and execute in a Node.js v6.11.5 environment. Because cloud functions execute in a Node.js environment, you can easily build and test the function on any Node.js environment before deploying.

Some examples of using cloud functions are file upload events to cloud storage, an incoming message on a specific application that triggers an event, or a simple log change. Events can also include database changes, files added to storage, or even new virtual machines being created.

We will briefly look at deploying a sample function using the GCP console:

1. Click on the top menu and select **Cloud Functions**.
2. Click on **Create function**:

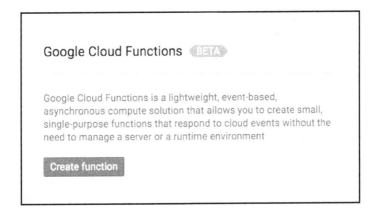

3. Google creates a sample function with code for you to test the functionality. Ideally you would use the `gcloud` tool or the SDK to create and deploy functions:

4. Select a name and the **Memory allocated** for the function. Depending on the complexity of the function, you may need to allocate more memory.

5. Choose a **Trigger** for the function. You can pick from an **HTTP** trigger, **Cloud Pub/Sub** topic, or a **Cloud Storage** bucket. We will discuss **Cloud Pub/Sub** topics and **Cloud Storage** buckets in the upcoming chapters.

6. The **URL** is how you can access this function.

7. The Javascript code is pre-written to test the function. The code here responds to an HTTP request that can provide a message field in its body.

8. Click Save to create the function:

9. Click on the function to open its dashboard. Here you can look at many aspects of this function including its invocations per second, memory usage, and execution time:

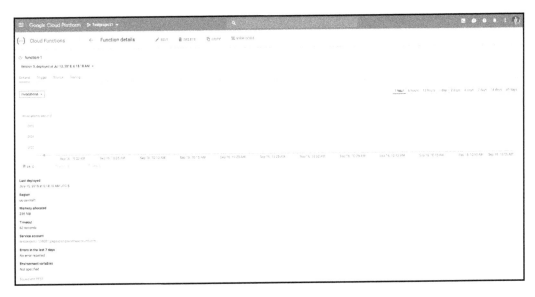

Functions on Dashboard

10. You can click **EDIT** to change the code of the function. Once saved your updated function is ready to be run. An additional feature is the ability to copy the function into a new function.

11. It is easy to test this function. Click on **Test function** to test the function:

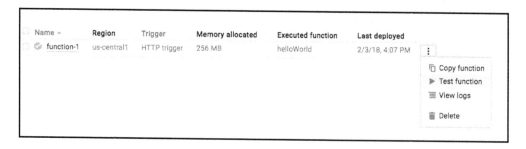

12. Enter `"message":"hello world"` in the { } and click **Test the function**:

Summary

In this chapter, we learned about Google's virtual machine capabilities using the compute engine, which allows you to deploy a rich set of virtual machines with a variety of features. We then looked at the app engine, which provides a PaaS environment that allows you to deploy your application using an SDK. Kubernetes engine is a powerful container orchestration and cluster management feature that allows you to deploy, manage, and scale your containers' workloads. Google Cloud Functions provide a serverless execution environment that lets you deploy your single-purpose functions into the cloud without the need to build, manage, and maintain a deployment environment or infrastructure. Cloud functions can react or be invoked using triggers that are tied to your cloud infrastructure or applications. In the next chapter, we will look into different storage options provided by GCP. We will learn more about persistent storage, local SSDs, and Google cloud storage buckets.

Google Cloud Platform Storage

3

In this chapter, we will look at GCP storage options and services. GCP has a strong suite of storage offerings that will meet your needs for structured, unstructured, transactional, and relational data. We have often seen, in previous chapters, that persistent storage is attached to your compute instances. We will begin this chapter by learning a bit more about persistent storage, local SSDs, and Google Cloud Storage buckets.

In this chapter, we will cover:

- Persistent storage
- Google Cloud Storage buckets
- Google Cloud Spanner
- Google Cloud SQL
- Google Cloud Bigtable

Persistent storage

Persistent storage consists of persistent disks that are durable network storage devices that are mapped to your instance. This logo represents persistent storage:

These disks can be used as regular storage disks and the data stored on them remains on the disk until it is deleted. The data on a persistent disk is redundant and also optimized for performance. Persistent disks are independent of any compute instances (virtual machines), so you can detach and re-attach a persistent disk to another compute instance. If your instance is deleted, your persistent disk data remains if you choose not to delete it. Persistent disks are offered in standard hard disk drives or solid state drives and can be resized at any time. Here is an example of a boot persistent disk for a Debian VM:

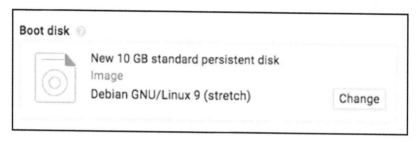

A compute engine, by default, gets deployed with one root persistent disk that contains the operating system. You can add more persistent disks when your application needs more disk storage space. The scope of persistent disks is limited to a zone, that is a persistent disk can only exist in one zone in a region and does not span multiple zones or regions. The redundancy, partitioning, and disk management tasks are handled by the compute engine. Instances write data to persistent disks three times in parallel to achieve a high rate of redundancy.

 Consider one persistent disk per partition instead of having multiple partitions on a single persistent disk. For additional partitions, add additional persistent disks.

As mentioned earlier, persistent disks are available as both standard hard disk drives and **solid state drives** (**SSD**). If your application requires high IOPS, SSD persistent disks are the best to use:

 Persistent disks are network-based disks and each write adds to the total network egress cap of your compute virtual machine instance.

1. To add more persistent disks during virtual machine creation, click on **Add item** as shown here:

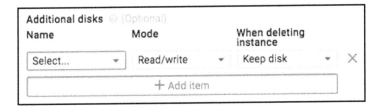

2. Select **Create a disk** from the dropdown.
3. Next, select the type of disk. You can also select an image or a snapshot to deploy the disk from:

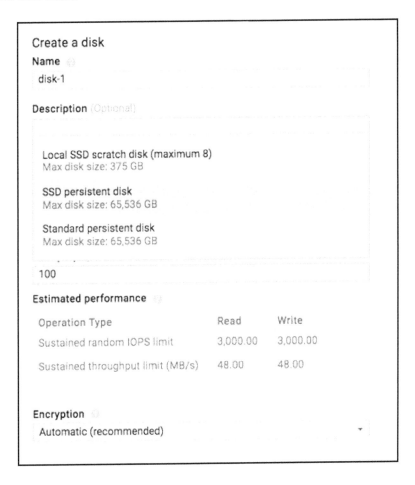

You can take snapshots on persistent disks to protect data against user error. Snapshots are incremental and allow you to take backups even while the instance is up and running.

All data is encrypted by the compute engine before it travels outside your virtual machine and is written on the persistent disk. Each persistent disk is encrypted either by the system defined or customer supplied keys. Once you delete a persistent disk, Google discards its cipher keys and that data is irretrievable.

The maximum size of a persistent disk is 64 TB. Most virtual machine instances can have up to a maximum of 64 TB of persistent disk storage space and a maximum of 16 attached disks. Custom machine instances with less than 3.75 GB of memory are limited to 3 TB of total persistent disk space and a maximum of four attached disks. Remember that the total persistent disk space of virtual machines includes the size of the root disk.

 Attaching more than 16 persistent disks is available in the beta feature where you can go up to 128 attached persistent disks for predefined machine types.

Another option in persistent disks is to the ability to use **local SSDs** that are physically attached to the server that hosts your virtual machine instance. Such a design gives you disks with higher throughput and lower latency than the standard or SSD (network based) persistent disks. Local SSDs connect through both SCSI and NVMe interfaces. Using a local SSD also does not count towards your network egress bandwidth cap.

There is a catch that the data on the local SSDs only lasts as long as the instance is up and running. Data will remain in the local SSD if you reboot the instance or if you live migrate the instance. During a live migration, all data from the local SSD is copied to the instance itself and you will notice a performance decrease. If the instance is stopped or deleted, all data is lost.

Local SSDs need to be manually stripped into a single logical volume to achieve best performance. Each local SSD disk is 375 GB in size and you can attach up to 8 local SSD disks to give you a total of 3 TB of storage space per instance.

Google Cloud Storage buckets

For applications that do not have low latency requirements, cloud storage buckets are the answer. Google Cloud Storage buckets form an object storage system that offers a very flexible, reliable, and scalable storage option for a compute engine instance. Cloud storage buckets also make it possible to share instance data across multiple instances and zones. You can also use cloud storage buckets as a common storage between your on-premise instances, as well as other cloud service providers. This logo represents Google Cloud Storage buckets:

Performance of cloud storage buckets depends on the location of the bucket relative to your instance and also the storage class that you select. There are four storage classes that you can select your cloud storage bucket from. The four storage classes are multi-regional storage, regional storage, nearline storage, and coldline storage. While all storage classes offer the same throughput and low latency, they differ primarily in their availability, minimum storage durations, and pricing.

 To use a cloud storage bucket in an instance, you need to use the Google Cloud Storage **Filesystem in Userspace** (**FUSE**) tool, which is an open source adapter for mounting cloud storage buckets. The mounted bucket behaves as a persistent disk and has a higher latency.

Multi-regional storage is geo-redundant storage that is appropriate for frequently accessed data. The geo-redundant feature ensures that cloud storage stores your data redundantly in at least two geographically separate locations. It is important to remember that geo-redundancy occurs asynchronously but cloud storage ensures that you have at least one copy redundant as soon as you upload your data. This storage class also offers a 99.95% availability SLA. Note that multi-regional storage is available in select locations.

The regional storage class is appropriate for storing data in the same regional location and does not offer the redundancy features that multi-regional storage does. Having data stored within a region results in better performance. Regional storage offers a 99.90% availability SLA.

The nearline storage class is ideal for storing data that is accessed rarely, for example, once a month. Ideally, backups and archival storage are some of the well known use cases for the nearline storage class. The nearline storage class offers a 99.0% availability SLA, and also carries a data retrieval costs along with a 30-day minimum storage duration.

While nearline storage class is ideal for infrequently accessed data, coldline storage is ideal for rarely accessed data such as archives and archival backups. Coldline storage offers long term archival storage at the lowest cost. Coldline storage offers a 99.0% availability SLA and data retrieval costs along with a 90-day minimum storage duration:

> If no storage class is selected, the default storage class for the bucket is **standard storage**. This standard storage class is equal to a multi-regional storage class if the bucket is in a location where multi-regional storage is supported. Standard storage is equivalent to regional storage when the bucket is in a regional location.

1. To create a bucket, select **Storage** from the side pane and click on **Browser**. Select **Create** to create a bucket:

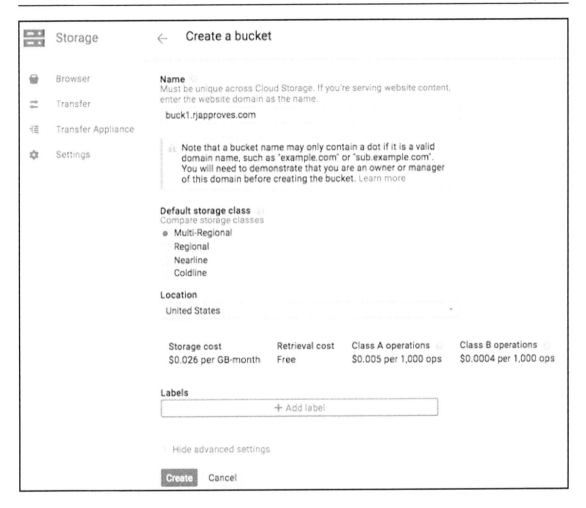

 You can even transfer data from your Amazon S3 instance or from any other HTTP/HTTPS instance or third party storage buckets into a **Google Cloud Storage bucket**. This option is ideal for data that is less than 20 TB in size.

2. Select **Transfer** to configure and initiate transfer of data from third party storage. You can even transfer data from one Google storage bucket to another:

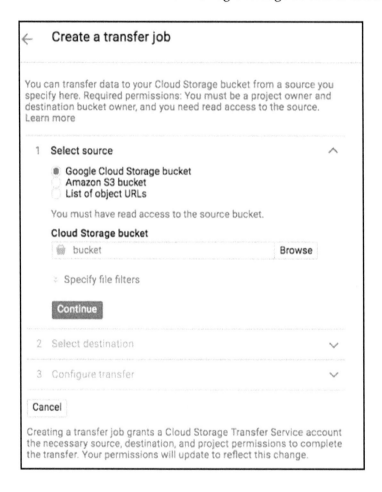

For buckets that are larger than 20 TB in size, a transfer appliance is recommended that can securely migrate data from one bucket to another. Currently, the appliance is provided on a per-request basis, and the form is shown here:

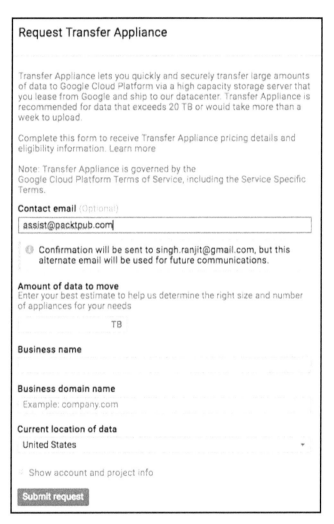

Google Cloud Spanner

Google Cloud Spanner is a fully managed relational database service. The service allows you to deploy mission critical databases and offers transactional consistency globally, along with automatic synchronous replication for high availability. Cloud spanner is ideal for mission critical databases that require replication and strong transactional consistency. This logo represents Google Cloud Spanner:

Cloud spanner databases are replicated synchronously; this is done at a global scale. The underlying operating system that powers cloud spanner has the ability to synchronously replicate at a byte level. Cloud spanner stores the databases as a bunch of files and the filesystem takes care of replicating these files across multiple regions. Cloud spanner stores all data as rows and replicates these rows on to multiple regions for high availability.

Cloud spanner uses a Paxos-based replication scheme where voting replicas participate in a vote for every write request before committing that request. This makes it possible for data to be read from any node of your cloud spanner instance simultaneously. It is also important to know that there are three types of replicas—read-write replica, read-only replica, and witness replicas. Witness and read-only replicas come into play in a multi-region configuration.

Read-write replicas maintain full copy of your data and support both read and write operations. These are also the only type of replicas used in a single-region configuration. Single-instance replicas only support reads and maintain a full replicated copy for your data from the read-write replicas. Witness replicas do not maintain a full copy of your data and participate in voting to commit writes.

 Leader election and voting concepts are out of the scope of this book. Refer to the GCP documentation at `https://cloud.google.com/spanner/docs/instances` to learn more.

With cloud spanner, when properly deployed, each node can provide up to 10,000 **queries per second** (**QPS**) of reads and 2,000 queries per second of writes. These, however, can vary depending on your workload and schema design.

Let's briefly look at deploying a cloud spanner instance:

1. Select **Spanner** from the left pane and click **Create an instance** to get started:

2. Now that we have created an instance, let's go ahead and create a simple database:

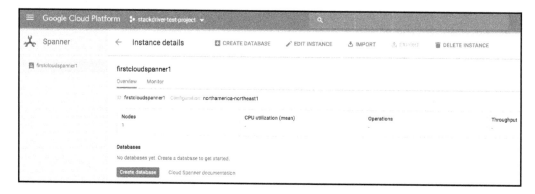

3. Click on **Create database**. You can name a table and add columns to your database, or use an SQL statement to create the table.

4. Sliding **Edit as text** lets you write SQL statements to build your database schema:

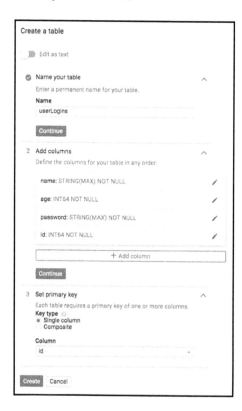

5. Click on **Create** to create the table in your database:

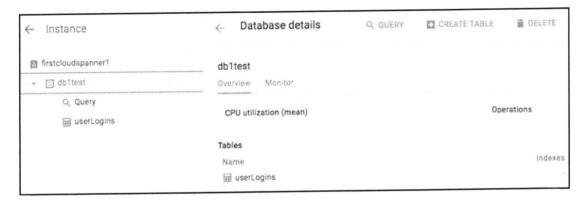

Google Cloud SQL

Cloud SQL is a fully managed relational database service for PostgreSQL and MySQL in the cloud. Cloud SQL offers many features for both MySQL and PostgreSQL databases. With cloud SQL, you can deploy large instances of your MySQL databases. These instances support MySQL 5.6 or 5.7 and up to 416 GB of RAM and 10 TB of storage space. Google also automatically encrypts all customer data on these database instances. The encryption also extends to Google's internal networks and temporary files. Cloud SQL also offers data replication across multiple zones and instances. This logo represents Google Cloud SQL:

Cloud SQL offers similar features for its PostgreSQL databases. As of this writing, PostgreSQL version 9.6 is supported with machines of up to 416 GB of RAM, 32 CPUs, and 10 TB of storage space, with room to grow in the future.

When a cloud SQL instance is deployed, Google charges you for the costs of the instance, storage, and network usage. In addition to these, for a PostgreSQL database, there is a CPU and memory pricing for dedicated core instances.

Let's look briefly at deploying a cloud SQL instance:

1. Select **SQL** in the left menu pane and click **Create an instance**:

2. **Choose a database engine** and click **Next** to pick from the two types of **MySQL** instances:

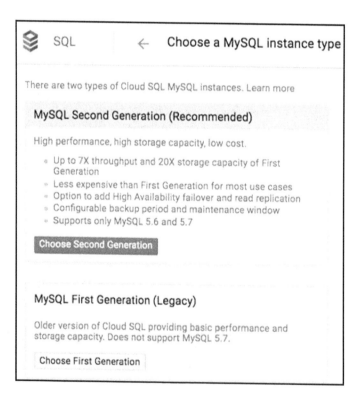

Instance creation hereafter is pretty straightforward:

3. Clicking on **Configuration options** allows for further customization:

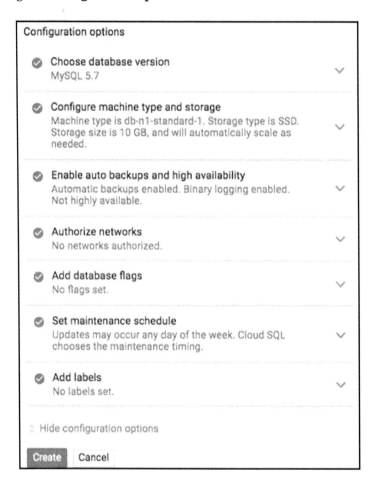

4. Click **Create** to create your instance. Once your instance is created, click on the instance name to view its dashboard:

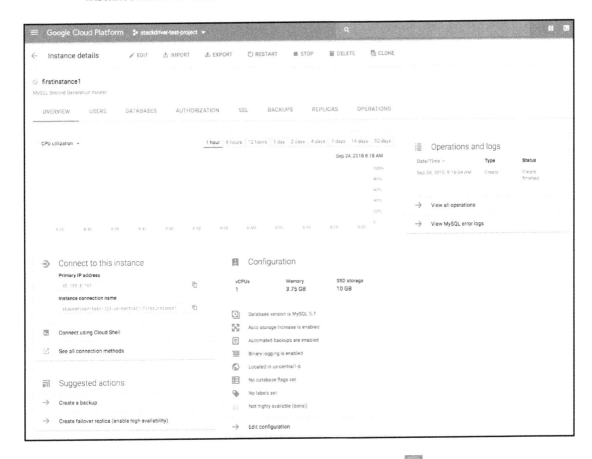

You can connect to the instance using cloud shell. Click on the ▣ icon on the right corner to start your cloudshell console on your GCP UI.

Once in cloud shell, use the built-in MySQL client to connect to your instance:

```
gcloud sql connect [INSTANCE_ID] --user=root
```

Here, instance ID is the one you used to create your instance. You will be prompted for a password once you run this command.

I created a couple of databases in my session. Try and identify them:

```
MySQL [(none)]> show databases;
+--------------------+
| Database           |
+--------------------+
| information_schema |
| myUserProfile      |
| mysql              |
| performance_schema |
| userInfo_1         |
+--------------------+
5 rows in set (0.00 sec)

MySQL [(none)]>
```

Google Cloud Bigtable

Cloud Bigtable is a petabyte scale NoSQL big data database service that can scale to billions of rows and thousands of columns. Ideal for applications that require high throughput, Cloud Bigtable is a perfect storage engine for batch MapReduce operations and machine learning applications. Cloud Bigtable stores data in tables, each of which is a sorted key/value map. The service is also equipped with multiple client libraries that allow you to easily integrate into existing environments. This logo represents cloud Bigtable:

Bigtable is widely used by Google for its internal projects as well. Many products at Google, such as web indexing, Google Earth, and YouTube rely on Bigtable.

Let's briefly look at deploying a Bigtable instance:

1. Select **Bigtable** from the side menu and click on **Create an instance**. The instance is a container for your cluster.

2. Enter the name and pick between production (three nodes minimum) or a development instance. Click **Create** when done:

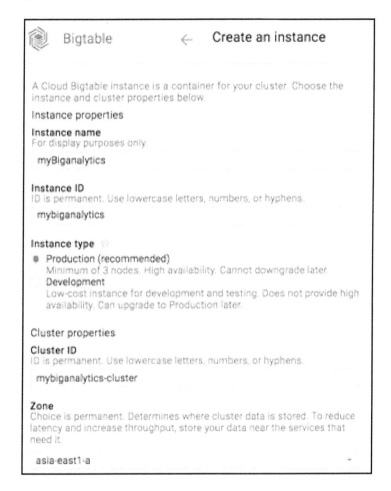

Bigtable: Creating an instance

3. Once your instance is created, click on the instance name to view its dashboard:

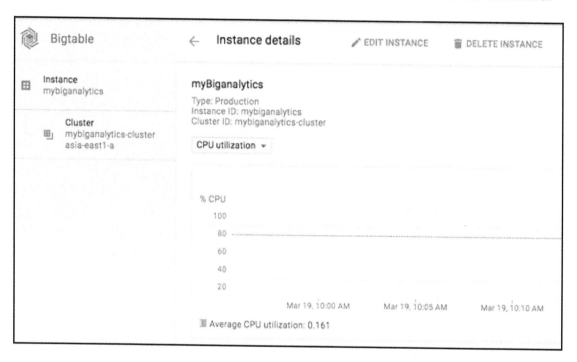

You can now use Google Cloud Dataproc (Google's fully managed service for running Apache Hadoop and Apache Spark) to use your Bigtable instance.

Summary

In this chapter, we have briefly looked at multiple storage options offered by the GCP. We started the chapter by discussing and deploying persistent storage to compute engine virtual machines. Next, we discussed cloud storage and the concept of buckets. Buckets are an object storage service and can offer low latency and flexibility. We also discussed cloud spanner, which is a fully managed relational database service. This is similar to the Google Cloud SQL service with the difference being that cloud SQL supports only MySQL and PostgreSQL engines. We ended the chapter by briefly looking at Google Cloud Bigtable, which is a petabyte scale NoSQL database service.

4
Google Cloud Platform Networking

In this chapter, we will cover:

- VPC networks
- Firewall rules
- VPC peering
- Private Google access
- Other networking concepts

In this chapter, we will discuss GCP VPC networking. Google offers lower latency and superior VPC networking capabilities than its competitors. We will begin the chapter by looking at VPC networks, firewall rules, and routing. We will also discuss an interesting concept of VPC peering and how it can help you connect multiple VPC networks to behave as an internal RFP 1918 environment. We will then look into other special configurations such as Private Google access. Before we end the chapter, we will briefly discuss other networking concepts of GCP.

VPC networks

VPC—a Google virtual network that acts and behaves just like a physical network in a data center. VPC provides the connectivity for your virtual machine instances in the compute engine, your Kubernetes engine clusters, and other resources that you may have. Every project that you create gets a default virtual network, which has one subnet assigned to each region, and you can create more virtual networks depending on your needs. This is how the VPC network logo looks:

When you create a VPC network, its scope is global, that is, VPC networks are not tied down or associated to a specific zone or a region. While the VPC network, all routes and associated firewall rules are global, the subnetworks (subnets) created are limited to the region. All resources created within a VPC can talk to each other using the internal private IP addresses, provided they are not blocked by firewall rules. Your instances can also talk to Google's API by using private IP addresses if you enable Private Google access to them.

 Private Google access allows an instance to communicate with Google's APIs over internal private IP addressing, instead of a public IP address.

It is important to note that VPC networks only support IPv4 unicast traffic. Multicast, broadcast or IPv6 traffic is not supported by VPC networks. You can, however, use IPv6 addresses to reach resources in a VPC network. For example, if your server needs a database, you can deploy the server in a datacenter that supports IPv6 while the database can be deployed in GCP. The server can communicate with the database that is configured with a IPv4 address.

 Core networking concepts such as routing and subnets are outside the scope of this book.

You can further divide a VPC into subnets that are partitions in a network. These subnets are associated with a particular region and more than one subnet can be created in a region. It is important to note that there are two types of VPC networks—auto mode and custom mode. When an auto mode VPC is created, one subnet is automatically created inside each region using predefined IP ranges that fit within a `10.128.0.0/9` block. In a custom mode VPC network, no subnets are created and it is up to you to create your own subnets in the IP ranges that best suit your needs. You will have complete control over the subnets in a custom mode VPC network. The default in each project is auto mode VPC networks and these can be converted to a custom mode VPC network but this action cannot be reversed.

When creating an instance, you select a zone, a network, and a subnet. The subnets you will see here are restricted to the region where you are deploying that instance. These allocations are subject to resource quota limits applicable to VPC networks. These limits cannot be increased:

Item	Quota or limit	Amount
VPC Networks per project	Quota	5
VM Instances per VPC network	Limit	7,000
VM Instances per subnet	No separate limit	

Let's look at an example to create a VPC network called `vpc-network1`:

1. Log in to your Google Cloud console and click on **VPC Network** in the side menu. You will see a default VPC network. This default network does count against your quota so you can delete it and create a new one.

2. Click on **Create a VPC network**:

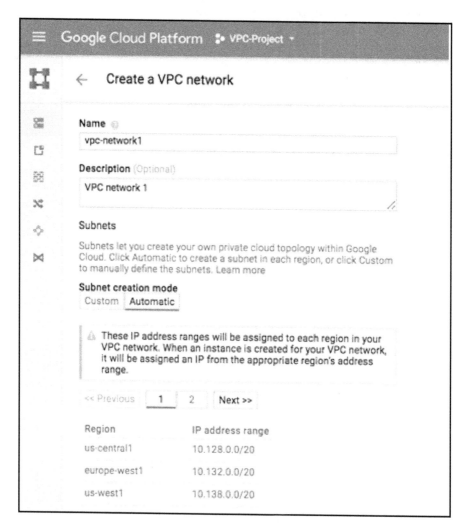

3. Here, selecting **Automatic** subnet creation will automatically assign an IP address range in all the regions. When you deploy resources in any of these regions, Google will assign that resource an IP address from this predefined range.

4. If you want to create a custom subnet, click on the **Custom** tab to select a **Region** and define your own subnet range:

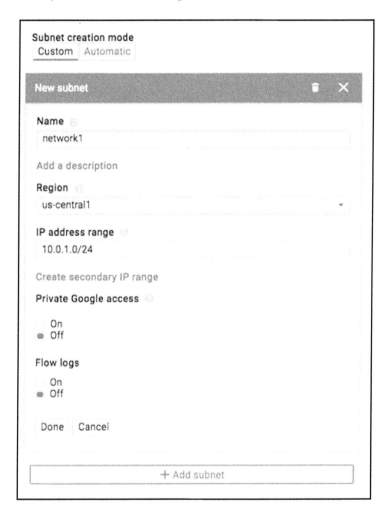

5. You can enable **Private Google access**, which gives you access to Google APIs from your internal IP address without the need to have public access. You can also add multiple custom subnets as needed.

6. You can select any firewall rules that apply to your environment. These rules are readily available to create your environment in a secure way.

7. Next, select **Dynamic routing mode**, where the **Regional** option allows cloud routers to learn routes in the region they are created, and the **Global** option allows you to dynamically learn routes from all regions over a single VPN. The routing option here only applies when a cloud router is deployed and is in use.

8. Click **Create** when done to create your VPC network. (We selected the **Automatic** subnet creation mode.):

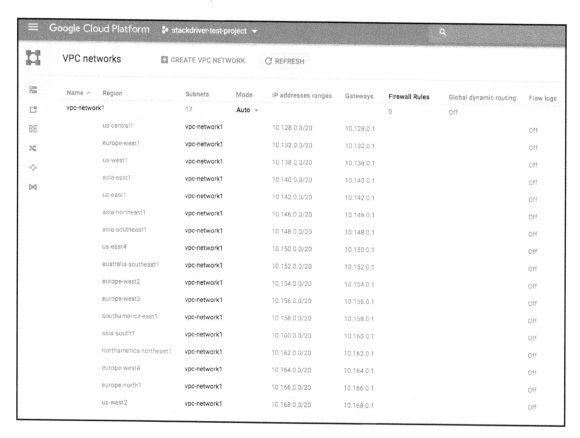

I also went ahead and created another VPC network called `vpc-network2` with two custom subnets, one is `us-central1` region and the other is `europe-west1` region:

Let's briefly look at some of the other networking features:

External IP addresses allows you to **Reserve a static address** in a region and attach it to a virtual machine instance or a load balancer instance:

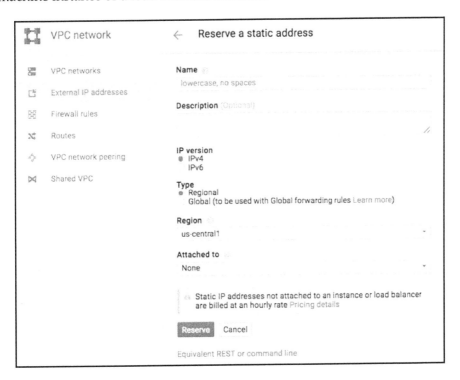

Let's explore the rest of the menu as we learn more about each one of these features.

Routes

Let's look into routing within the GCP. As a reminder, this section does not cover the basics of network routing in general but talks about how routes are defined within the GCP environment. A route is a networking mapping of an IP range to its destination. Every network in GCP has routes in places that allow an instance to send traffic to each other or even across multiple subnets across different regions. Along with these routes, every network has a default route that directs traffic to outside the network. If you want to change the default route, you can do so by overriding it with a custom static route. If a route is in place, the only way to prevent an instance from talking to another instance is by using firewall rules. We will learn more about firewall rules in the next section.

When you create a VPC network, a default route for internet traffic (0/0) is created. For each subnet you create, one route is created for all local traffic and also for communication of instances between multiple subnets within a VPC network. If you create a static route for an IP address range that overlaps with the subnet's IP address range, then such a static route is automatically disabled. GCP does this to protect inter-vm communication within a VPC network.

It is important to note that every route has a priority value associated with it. This priority value is used to break ties in cases where there is more than one matching route. A lower value is higher priority, so a priority of 100 gets precedence over a priority value of 200. The default priority value is 1,000.

 For any packets that are being routed and sent to the internet, the instance must have a public IP address. If there is a route that routes all your private instance traffic to an internet gateway, such packets will be dropped because your instance does not have a public IP address.

Click on **Routes** to list all the current routes in place for your VPC network. You can click on **Create a route** to create a custom route for a specific network. This route can have its next hop, a default gateway, or even a VPN tunnel:

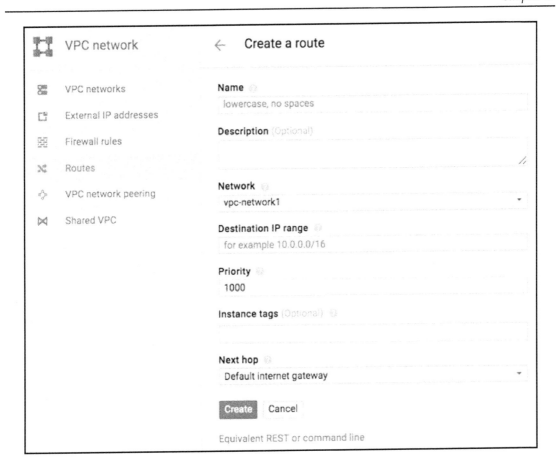

Firewall

Firewall rules in GCP let you allow or deny traffic based on rules you apply to your instances. Firewall rules are applied at a networking level with every VPC network acting as a distributed firewall. Even though firewall rules are applied at a networking level, they allow/deny connections at an instance level. The advantage of a distributed firewall is that it does not only filter traffic between instances but also filters traffic between networks. All firewall rules are specific to a VPC network with each rule either allowing or denying traffic.

Firewall rules, being unique to a VPC network, cannot be shared between multiple VPC networks. It is important to note that firewall rules in GCP only support IPv4 traffic. There is also no logging mechanism for firewall rules; this means that you cannot log an **Allow** or a **Deny** action in the firewall. The GCP firewall allows bidirectional traffic once a session is established, meaning that GCP firewall rules are stateful. By default, every VPC network has an implied egress rule and an implied deny ingress rule. The egress rule ensures all outbound traffic while the ingress rule protects all instances by blocking incoming traffic to them. These two default rules cannot be removed and have the lowest priority value of 65535.

There are other rules that are in place for the default network. These rules allow incoming traffic to instances. Some of these rules are default-allow-internal, default-allow-ssh, default-allow-rdp, and default-allow-icmp. GCP also permanently blocks some of the traffic types. These permanently blocked rules cannot be removed. Some of the blocked traffic types include GRE traffic and protocols other than TCP, UDP, ICMP, and IPIP. The rules also permanently block egress traffic on TCP port 25 and egress traffic on TCP port 465 or 587.

Each firewall rule has a numerical priority that is used to determine whether the rule will be applied. The highest priority rule that matches the traffic is applied. The direction of traffic component of a rule describes whether the traffic is ingress or egress. The action or match component will determine whether to permit or deny traffic. The target component defines the instance to which the rule will apply. A source or a destination for ingress and egress rules. The components also include protocol and port. There is an enforcement status component as well that allows you to enable or disable the firewall rule without having to delete it.

The GCP firewall also has the ability to limit the source and target to GCP resources by using an IAM service account. Such a rule will apply to any new instances created by this service account and also existing instances if you updated their service account associations. Only one service account can be associated with an instance.

Let's check out what this looks like in the GCP portal.

Click on **Firewall rules** to enable rules to control incoming and outgoing traffic to an instance. Firewall rules are applied to all subnets on a network:

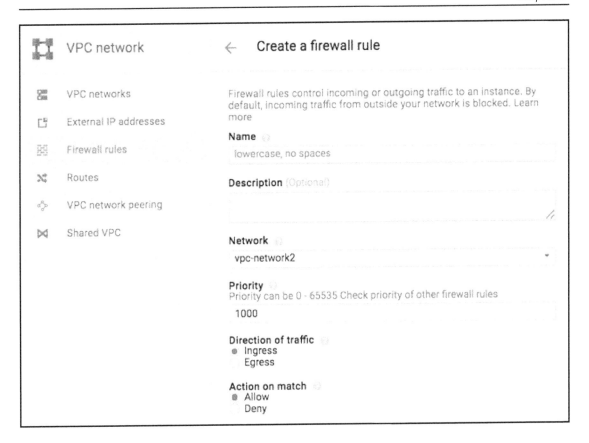

VPC network peering

The VPC network peering allows private (RFC 1918) connectivity across two VPC networks that can span over multiple projects and even multiple organizations. In an organization with multiple network administrative domains, VPC peering allows for services to be available across VPC networks in a private IP space. These organizational services can also be exposed to other organizations via this private space. VPC network peering has more advantages than using public IP addresses or VPNs to connect organizations or networks with latency, and exposure to public internet being one of the most important ones. Also, when networks are peered, there are no egress traffic costs, which saves on overall network costs.

VPC network peering works with compute engine and app engine flexible environments. Routes, firewalls, VPNs, and other traffic tools are applied independently to each VPC network. When peering is set up, each side will only work when the configuration matches from both sides. Either side can turn off peering association at any time. One VPC network can peer with multiple VPC networks. It must be noted that the CIDR on one VPC network cannot overlap with the CIDR on another VPC network.

In the following diagram, you will see two projects, **P1** and **P2**, that have two virtual networks that are attempting to peer. This will be an invalid peering configuration because both the projects have overlapping subnets, which causes routing issues:

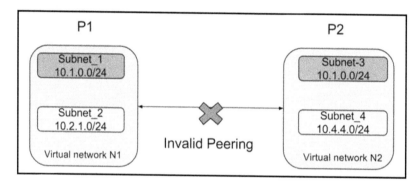

This scenario is also valid when there is more than one VPC network attempting to peer with an overlapping subnet in the peering chain. The following diagram illustrates this example, where project **P3** has an overlapping subnet with project **P1**:

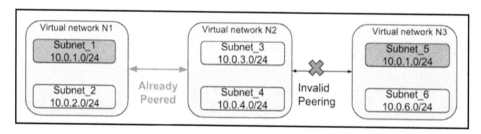

In an already peered network, GCP checks for any overlap when a new subnet is created. If there is an overlap, the new subnet creation will fail but the peering between the networks will not break. The following is an illustration of this subnet creation check. As you can see, virtual network **N2** has a new subnet, **Subnet_3**, that overlaps **Subnet_1** in virtual network, **N1**. GCP will check to ensure that there is no overlap during subnet creation and will take corrective action if there is overlap:

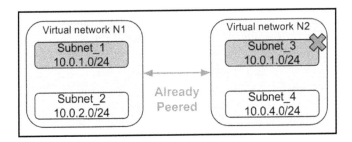

GCP also ensures this subnet overlap check happens when multiple networks are peered. In the following diagram, you will see subnet creation in virtual network **N3** will fail because of an overlapping subnet in virtual network **N1**. It is important to note that subnet creation will fail but not the peering:

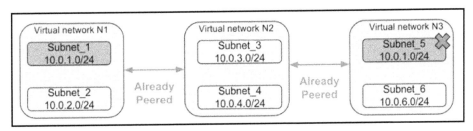

Some things to remember about VPC network peering:

- One VPC network can peer with multiple VPC networks. However, there is a limit. A network can have up to 25 directly peered networks that include both active and inactive peers.
- A VPC network can have up to 7,500 VM instances in itself and in all directly peered networks.
- An important point to remember is that only VPC networks are supported for peering and not legacy networks.
- Once you peer two networks, every internal private IP becomes accessible across the peered networks. This, in effect, becomes a huge private network with multiple subnets in place guided by firewall rules that can further restrict traffic, if need be. VPC peering does not provide specific routing controls so any filtering of traffic based on CIDRs is not possible. If any filtering is needed, firewall rules need to be in place to allow or deny traffic to specific IPs.

- When multiple VPC networks are connected, dissociative peering is not supported. This means if two networks are peered with a common network and are not peered directly with each other, they still cannot talk to each other. As an example, if **N1** is peered with **N2** and **N3** ,and **N2** and **N3** are not peered directly, then **N2** cannot talk to any instances in **N3**.
- An instance can have multiple network interfaces, each connected to a different VPC network.

Let's set up VPC peering:

1. I created two projects called **us-project1** and **asia-project1**. The aim here is to create two VPC networks in each of these regions and establish peering between them:

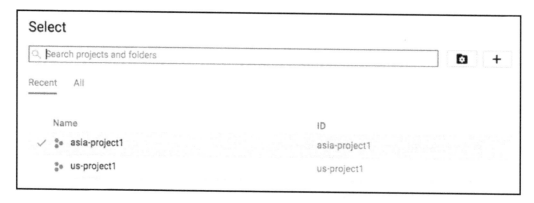

2. Let's create a VPC network under the **asia-project1** project. Let's call it **asia-vpc-network**. Select any Asia region for this VPC. Create this network with a `192.168.1.0/28` subnet:

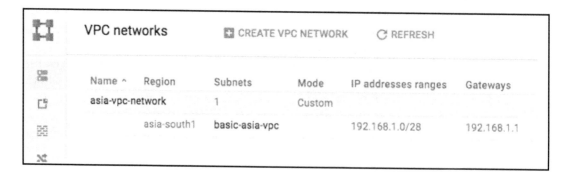

3. Now, let's create another VPC network under the **us-project1** project and call it **us-vpc-network**. Select any US region for this VPC. Create this network with a `192.168.2.0/28` subnet:

Remember that VPC peering does not work with overlapping subnets.

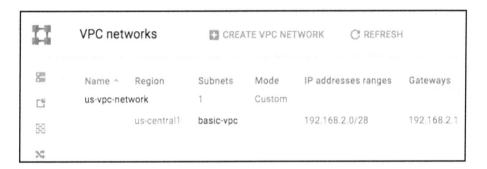

Now that we have established two VPC networks in two completely different regions, let's go ahead and peer them with each other.

Under the **us-project1** project:

1. Click on **VPC peering** on the left menu.
2. Click on **Create connection** from the introduction screen.
3. Make sure you note down the project ID for both the projects and also the VPC networks we wish to peer:

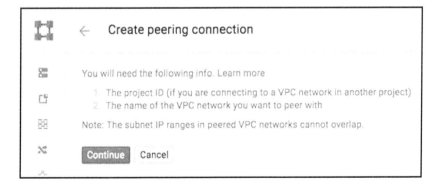

4. Click **Continue**.

5. Enter the following details:

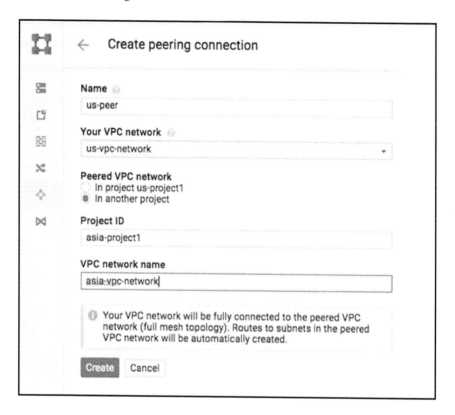

Remember your **Project ID** will be different to what I have. Also make sure the VPC network name matches exactly what you have created.

6. Click **Create**. The VPC on the US region is now created:

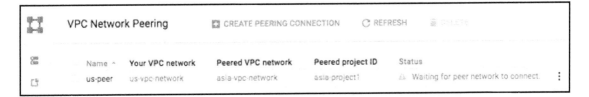

We now need to create the VPC from the Asia region to complete the connection:

1. Switch the project to **asia-project1** project and click on **VPC peering**.
2. Click on **Create connection** and click **Continue**:

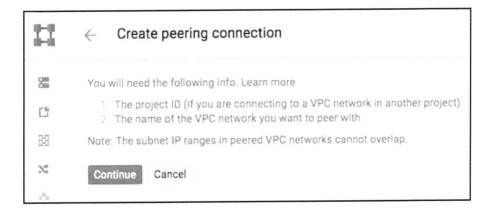

3. Fill out the VPC peering info and make sure you use your **Project ID** that was assigned to your project:

4. Click **Create**. You will immediately see a **Connected** status:

5. Check the VPC peering status in your other project. It should also show **Connected**.

We have successfully established the peering between two sites across two different continents. All resources deployed in these two VPC networks will be able to communicate with each other over internal networks.

Private Google access

By default, virtual machines instances that have an external IP address can access Google APIs. Not all instances will have a public IP address and your instances may need access to Google APIs and services. Private Google access allows your instances to reach Google APIs and services using an internal IP address rather than a public IP address. This makes it possible for you to use private access to allow virtual machines to reach Google services. Services such as BigQuery, Cloud Bigtable, container registry, Cloud Dataproc, cloud storage, and many more can all be reached internally through Private Google access.

You can enable Private Google access on a subnet level and any VMs on that subnet can access Google APIs by using their internal IP address. These subnets can either be auto or custom. Here is a list of services that can be accessed privately using this feature. Remember that this is a dynamic list so it can change as Google enables more services:

- BigQuery
- Cloud Bigtable
- Container registry
- Cloud Dataproc
- Cloud datastore
- Cloud pub/sub
- Cloud spanner
- Cloud storage

 Private Google access does not apply to cloud SQL. You do not get private connectivity.

If your VM instance has an external IP address, this remains unaffected and your VM can continue to access Google services and APIs on its internal IP address when Private Google access is enabled. It is also important to remember that DNS resolutions of Google domains does not change with Private Google access. Both internal and external IP addresses will resolve to external IP addresses of Google domains. For Private Google access to work properly, you also need to have a **default-internet-gateway** set in the VM instances so Google services can be reached. If you have routes configured to reach external IP addresses, then such a default internet gateway need not be set.

Google services reside on external IP addresses. For Private Google access to work, a **default-internet-gateway** needs to be set to allow access to those services from an internal IP.

Enabling **Private Google access** is as easy as selecting the option during creation of a subnet in a VPC network:

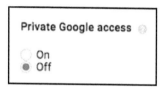

Other networking concepts

GCP offers many other networking tools and services that allow you to build and deploy an efficient environment in the cloud. We will look at these concepts briefly.

Load balancing

GCP offers load balancing and auto scaling for groups of instances. With load balancing, you can distribute incoming traffic to multiple virtual machine instances. This allows you to scale your application and handle heavy traffic more efficiently. The load balancer can also detect and remove unhealthy machines and re-add such instances when they become healthy.

GCP load balancer uses forwarding rules to match traffic types and forwards them to the load balancer. GCP offers the load balancer service as a managed service, which means if any components or if the load balancer fails, it will be restarted or replaced automatically.

GCP offers different types of load balancing. TCP proxy load balancing distributes TCP traffic among groups of virtual machine instances based on the proximity to the user. SSL proxy load balancing distributes SSL traffic and HTTP(s) load balancing distributes HTTP(s) traffic among different instances. GCP also allows for **regional external load balancing** that distributes network traffic among a pool of instances within a region. **Regional internal load balancing** distributes traffic from GCP virtual machine instances to a group of instances within the same region. It is important to note that regional internal load balancing distributes traffic internally.

Let's look at a high-level overview of creating a load balancer:

1. In the left dashboard tab, go to **Network services** and click on **Load balancing**. Click the **Create a load balancer** button on the introduction page:

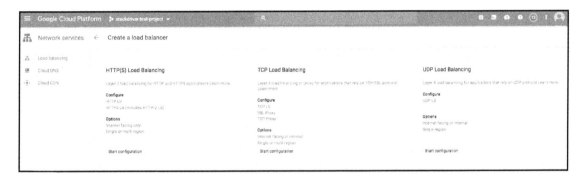

2. Click on **Start configuration** for any of the load balancers. In this example, I will use the **HTTP(S) Load Balancing**:

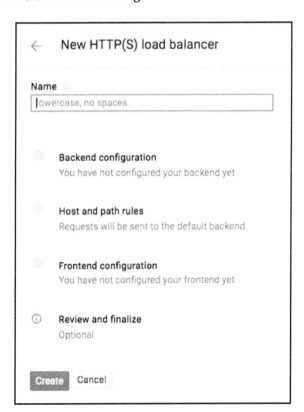

Configuring an HTTP(S) load balancer involves three steps: backend configuration, host and path rules, and frontend configuration. Each step helps you map the load balancer to backend resources, define the host and path rules that the load balancer will follow, and the frontend configuration such as IP address and ports.

Google Cloud CDN

Cloud **content delivery network (CDN)** stores content locally at certain edges and works with the HTTP(s) load balancing service to deliver this content to users. Google makes this happen with its global points of presence that are geographically located allowing content to be cashed closer to users. When a user requests content from a site hosted on GCP, the request arrives at an edge location of Google's network that is typically closer to the user. Cloud CDN caches at these locations, which improves the response times for the user should they request the same content again (before the CDN timeout expires). This is the CDN logo:

It is important to remember that not all data will be stored on the CDN. Whenever a user requests some content for the first time, the cache cannot fulfill the request. The cache might attempt to look for this content in a nearby cache. If it can find it, it will serve that content to the user and also store a local copy. If it does not find the content in a nearby cache, it will then send such a request to the HTTP(s) load balancer, which forwards it to one of the backend servers.

Google's caching mechanism also determines which content is more popular and ensures that it remains available while evicting content that is unpopular to conserve space. When some content is available in the cache, it is retrieved using a cache key and the cache responds directly to the user thereby giving a much faster response to the user's query.

Let's go over a high-level overview of what the cloud CDN feature looks like in GCP portal.

Click on **Cloud CDN** listed under the **Network services**. Click on **Add origin** on the introduction page:

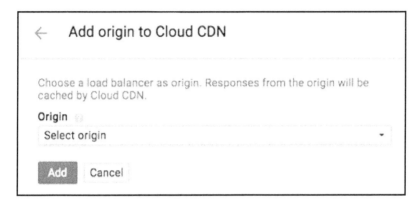

An origin is your server that responds to user requests. These responses are cached by the cloud CDN. Any server from where your data originates is an origin server.

Cloud VPN

Cloud VPN makes it possible for you to connect your on-premises network to your Google network using an IPSEC VPN tunnel. This connectivity is recommended for low-volume data and allows for encrypted traffic between your networks travels over the public internet. The encryption protects your data while keeping costs low as your data travels over the public internet. A cloud VPN is illustrated here:

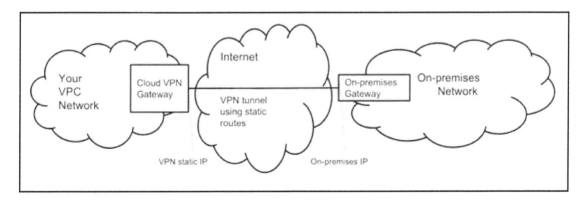

In this illustration, you will notice that on the left side you have your VPC network with a cloud VPN gateway. On the right side, you have your on-premises network that has a VPN gateway, which can either be a dedicated physical or a virtual gateway. The cloud VPN gateway makes it easy for you to connect these two networks securely over the public internet using a VPN tunnel.

Cloud VPN supports site-to-site VPN and one cloud VPN gateway can be connected to multiple on-premises networks. This means multiple on-premises networks can connect securely to a single VPC network and can have access to instances in that network. Cloud VPN uses a cloud router to support both static and dynamic routes for managing traffic between your sites. Cloud VPN is highly reliable and Google offers an SLA of 99.9% service reliability.

Ideally, an on-premises environment will have a dedicated physical or a virtual IPSEC VPN gateway, which can be configured to connect to a cloud VPN gateway endpoint. Cloud VPN only supports gateway-to-gateway scenarios and does not support client-to-gateway scenarios that are typically done using an SSL VPN client software. Cloud VPN also does not support other VPN technologies, only IPSEC is supported for now.

An important point to remember is that the on-premises CIDR IP range must not conflict with the CIDR range of the VPC network.

Cloud interconnect

Google's Cloud Interconnect makes it possible for you to connect your on-premises network directly to your VPC without traversing the public internet. This feature also provides RFC 1918 communication, making it possible to access internal private IPs directly across both networks. There are two ways you can consume cloud interconnect, **Google Cloud Interconnect - Dedicated** and **Google Cloud Interconnect - Partner**. The dedicated interconnect provides a direct physical connection between your on-premises network and Google's network while the partner interconnect provides connectivity between your network and Google's network through a service provider partner. The logo for Google's Cloud Interconnect looks like this:

Cloud interconnect is typically more efficient than having your traffic travel over the public internet. Because the connection is tied into Google's network, your traffic takes fewer hops to reach the resources and this means fewer packet drops. Cloud interconnect is ideal for high volume traffic with the dedicated Cloud Interconnect offering a maximum of 80 GBps of total capacity per interconnect while the partner interconnect can offer connection speeds ranging from 50 MBps to 10 GBps for each VLAN. Because of the dedicated nature of the setup, your network egress costs remain low, making it the most cost-effective method if you have high volume traffic. However, there are overhead costs associated with the setup of the cloud interconnect private/dedicated connections.

Summary

In this chapter, we looked at some of the networking concepts that are core to GCP. We looked at VPC networking and how it allows you to create networks and subnets in every region, as needed. Instances and resources in the region can be part of this VPC network and can automatically be assigned an internal IP address. All traffic within a VPC network can be restricted only via firewall rules. We also looked at VPC peering that lets you peer two VPC networks across two different projects. We briefly looked at other networking services offered by Google, such as load balancer, cloud CDN, cloud VPN, and cloud interconnect.

5
Google Cloud Platform Containers

In this chapter, we will look into Kubernetes and container management. We will begin the chapter by going over the core concepts of Kubernetes. Next, we will get our hands dirty by administering a Kubernetes cluster in GCP and performing different actions on it. We will also configure cluster networking and learn more about its different aspects and how they fit into this container world. This chapter has been written to give you a fairly good understanding of Kubernetes, but it is highly recommended that you read through some advanced books to become a true expert in Kubernetes.

In this chapter, we will cover:

- Kubernetes concepts
- Administering a cluster
- Configuring cluster networking

Kubernetes concepts

In the first chapter, we briefly looked at Kubernetes, its concepts, and even deploye a cluster. Before we dive deeper into Kubernetes, let's review it's concepts once again.

Kubernetes provides a managed environment for deploying and managing your containerized applications. Multiple Google Compute Engine instances are grouped together to form a container cluster that are managed by the Kubernetes engine. It is important to note that the Kubernetes engine only works with containerized applications. This means you must package your applications into containers before you deploy them on a Kubernetes engine. In Kubernetes, these containers are called **workloads**. At the time of this writing, Kubernetes only supports Docker containers.

Kubernetes is one of the most sought after skill in the market today.

The basic architecture of a Kubernetes engine is made up of a cluster master and worker machines called nodes. The master and the node machines together form the cluster orchestration system. The cluster master is the core of the Kubernetes engine and runs the control panel processes that include the API server, scheduler, and core resource controllers. The cluster master's API process is the hub of all communication as all interactions are done via the Kubernetes API calls. This makes the API server, the single source of truth for the entire cluster.

 The cluster master is the single source of truth for the entire cluster.

A container cluster typically contains one or more nodes, which are compute engine VMs called worker machines that run your containerized workloads. These compute virtual machines are of standard VM type with 1 virtual CPU and 3.75 GB of RAM, but these values are customizable. These nodes (worker machines) are automatically created by the Kubernetes engine when you create a cluster. The master controls each of these nodes and the Kubernetes engine can perform automatic repairs and upgrades on these cluster nodes. All necessary services to support Docker containers run on these nodes. The nodes also run the Kubernetes node agent (`Kubelet`), which communicates with the master and also starts and stops the containers.

One thing to remember is that every node has some resources allocated to run Kubernetes services, so there will be a difference in the node's total resources and the node's allocatable resources:

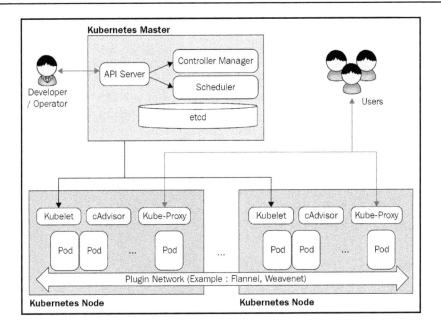

Let's describe the different components in this illustration:

- **Kubernetes master**: This functions as the API server receiving requests from developers. These requests can range from creating new container pods or adding more nodes (compute engine virtual machines).
- **etcd**: This functions as a backend system and is part of the API server that uses a distributed key-value system to store the cluster state. Ideally, etcd is run on a different machine to ensure availability.
- **Controller manager**: This has many controller functions such as the replication controller, endpoint controller, and namespace controller. The primary function of a controller manager is to watch over the shared state of the cluster and attempt to move it to the final state. For example, the replication controller ensures that there are a right number of replica pods running for each application.
- **Scheduler**: This takes care of pod placement on the nodes and ensures a balanced deployment.
- **Node components**: This run on every node that is part of the cluster. A node at a minimum contains the container runtime, such as Docker, to run the containers.
- **Kubelet service**: This executes containers (pods) on the node and ensures its health.
- **Kube-proxy**: This functions as a network proxy or load balancer that allows for service abstraction.

Kubernetes nodes run pods. A pod is the most basic object in Kubernetes. A pod can be one or more container but typically one container runs per pod. Multiple containers can be run in one pod and these containers together function as a single entity. In essence, a pod can be visualized as a self-contained logical host that has all the specific needs in place for a container to run. Pods also allow access to networking and storage resources to the container. Each pod automatically gets assigned a unique IP address and containers in the pod share this IP address and network ports.

It is important to remember that pods are ephemeral and once a pod is deleted, it cannot be recovered or brought back. If a host running multiple pods fails, that host is re-deployed and the controller determines if the pod needs to be deployed or not. Typically, you do not create or delete a pod. This is done by the controller deployed to manage the creation and deletion of pods. The controller manages the entire process for you, such as rolling updates for all pods.

Administering a cluster

Let's look at doing some hands-on labs to deploy our cluster. Our goal here is to deploy a simple Kubernetes cluster and review its different functions.

When you create a cluster, you specify the number of node instances. This number becomes the default node pool. A node pool is basically a grouping of nodes that are identical to each other. You can create multiple node pools if needed or add to the node pools if required. Node pools are useful when you need to schedule pods that require different sets of resources. For example, you can create a node pool of small compute instances and another node pool with SSD-backed storage instances. Node pools also allow you to make changes to nodes without affecting the entire cluster and other node pools:

1. Log in to your GCP account and create a new project called `KubeCluster`.
2. If this is the first time, Google Cloud will take some time to prepare and enable its backend API services.
3. Click on **CREATE CLUSTER**. What you are doing here is deploying a master and its nodes.
4. Pick a **Name** for the cluster. Pick either **Zonal** or **Regional** deployment. **Zonal** deployment is tied to a single zone in a region, while **Regional** deployment can spread the cluster's master VMs to multiple zones with-in a region for higher availability:

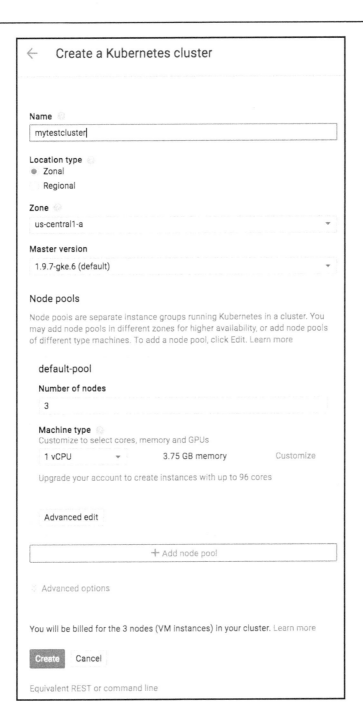

5. You can select the Kubernetes version type and set the machine **Size** and the number of nodes:

6. Click **Create** when done:

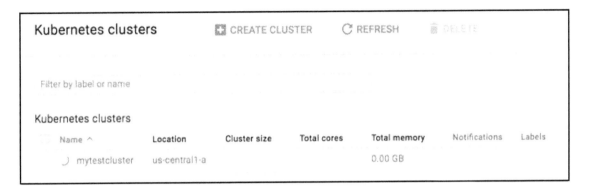

7. Our cluster is being deployed and will take a few minutes. When you click compute engine, you will see three nodes being deployed that form the default node pool:

8. In the **Instance groups**, you will notice a new instance group created with your Kubernetes cluster name. This group will have your three nodes in it:

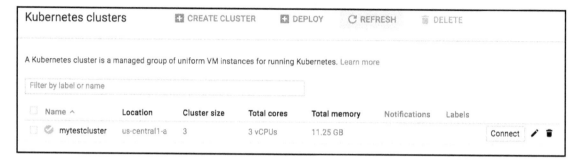

9. Clicking on the group shows the three nodes that are currently being deployed:

When your cluster is deployed, this is what you should see:

10. Click on the cluster to get more details and perform other actions such as upgrades and/or deletions:

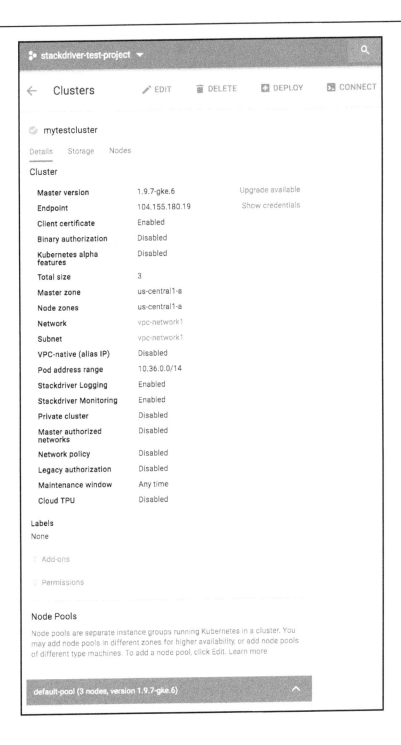

You see that the master version is **1.9.7-gke.6** and that an upgrade is available. Scrolling down shows you more details about your node pools:

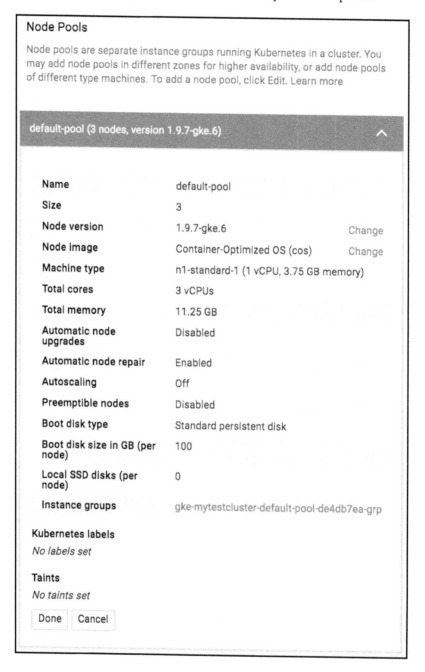

11. To add more node pools, you can click on **EDIT** and click on the **Add node pool** button.

Let's connect to our cluster:

1. Click on **CONNECT** which should give you the command line that you need to connect to your cluster. Remember that you need to have the Google Cloud SDK installed on your machine. You will also need the kubectl components installed for the Cloud SDK:

```
WARNING: Accessing a Kubernetes Engine cluster requires the kubernetes commandline
client [kubectl]. To install, run
  $ gcloud components install kubectl
```

2. Once done, you can run the command in the popup:

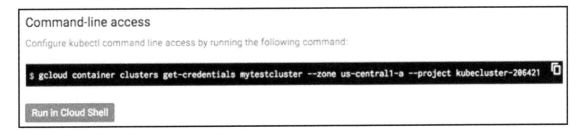

This gets the credentials and stores them, so now you can run the kubectl commands and manage the cluster.

Let's first deploy some workloads:

1. In the side panel menu under **Kubernetes**, click on the **Workloads**.

2. Here you can deploy workloads. Also, take a moment to look at the system
   workloads and review the different system workloads that make Kubernetes run:

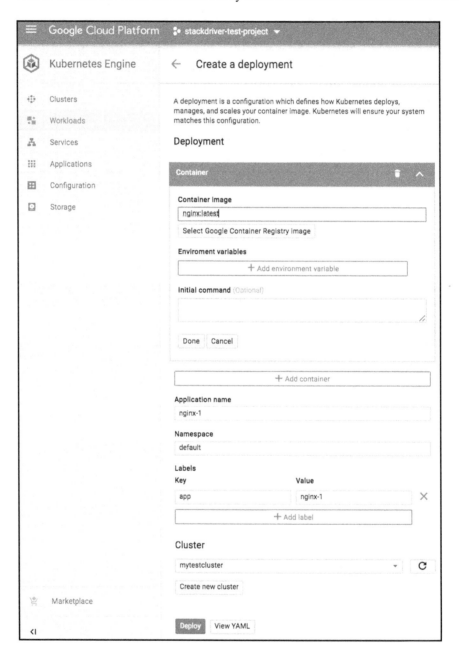

3. Clicking on **Deploy** shows the deployment pane. I will simply pick the defaults in place and click **Deploy**. You can add more containers (pods or workloads) to this deployment or stay with the default `nginx:latest` deployment. For custom images, you can upload them into the container registry.

4. Once deployed, you will see your containers (workloads or pods) deployed and in a running state:

At this point, you are considered to have a deployment, which is a replicated, **stateless** application on your cluster. You can create **stateful** applications as well. Stateful applications save the internal state of the application and require a **persistent storage** mapped to your pods. A container's root filesystem is not suitable for storing persistent data. Remember that containers are disposable entities and based on a scenario, a cluster manager may delete or reschedule any container at any time. Any data stored locally on a container will be lost and is not suitable for storing a state of an application.

This is why we create `PersistentVolume` (**PV**) and `PersistentVolumeClaims` (**PVC**) to store persistent data. A PV is a storage unit in a cluster that can be dynamically provisioned by Kubernetes or manually provisioned by an administrator. Persistent volumes are backed by GCP persistent disk or an NFS share and so on. A `PersistentVolumeClaim` is a request for storage by a user that can be filled by a `PersistentVolume`. For example, if a persistent volume is 250 GB, a user can create a `PersistentVolumeClaim` of 10 GB if that is all his application needs. This claim can now be mapped to a mount points in a pod (container or workload).

The important thing to remember is that `PersistentVolumes` and `PersistentVolumeClaims` are independent of a pod's life cycle. Events such as restarts and deletions of pods will not delete any persistent data stored on these volumes. For the most part, you will not have to create `PersistentVolumes` and `PersistentVolumeClaims` separately. Kubernetes will automatically provision a persistent disk for you when you create a `PersistentVolumeClaim`.

Let's create a `PersistentVolume` and a `PersistentVolumeClaim` using Kubernetes. To do this open your terminal so we can write a YAML file and use the `kubectl` commands to execute it:

```
      kind: PersistentVolumeClaim
  apiVersion: v1
  metadata:
      name: myvolumeclaim
  spec:
      accessModes:
       - ReadWriteOnce
      resources:
            requests:
      storage: 250Gi
```

Save this code in a file with the name `pvc.yaml`.

In the terminal, type:

```
$ kubectl apply -f pvc.yaml
persistentvolumeclaim "myvolumeclaim" created
$ kubectl get pvc
NAME            STATUS    VOLUME                                        CAPACITY   ACCESS MODES   STORAGECLASS   AGE
myvolumeclaim   Bound     pvc-3d7fedf7-6bfa-11e8-a49e-42010a800112     250Gi      RWO            standard       8s
```

You can now see a volume claim is created with a volume and is 250 GB in size. Kubernetes automatically created this disk for us when we requested the claim be created. This reduces management. It also has `ReadWriteOnce` access and the storage class is standard. This is the default storage class if no storage class is specified.

Three different access modes are supported:

- `ReadWriteOnce`: The volume can be mounted as a read-write by a single node
- `ReadOnlyMany`: The volume can be mounted as a read-only by many nodes
- `ReadWriteMany`: The volume can be mounted as read-write by many nodes; volumes backed by compute engine persistent disks do not support this mode

Under the Kubernetes engine, click on **Storage**. You will see a PVC created called **myvolumeclaim**:

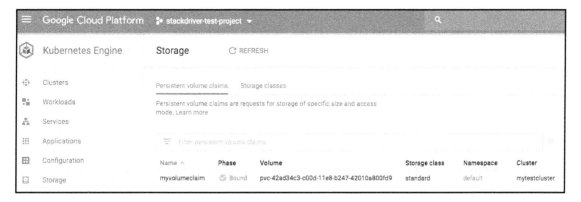

The **Storage classes** tab shows the storage class information:

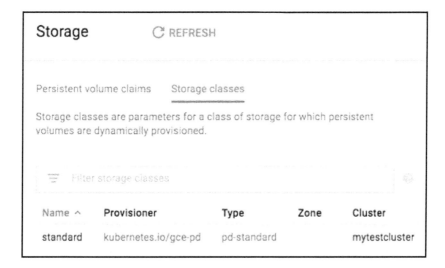

Go back to your **Kubernetes clusters** view and click on your cluster. Go to the **Storage** tab:

You can see that **Persistent volumes** has been provisioned. Now, any new container that gets deployed will have this volume presented to it and have access to all the data.

Notice the **active revisions** with a revision number and a name. This is the replica set. A replica set ensures that a number of pod replicas are running at a time. You can define the minimum desired and maximum replicas and Kubernetes will ensure that the pods are deployed to satisfy those conditions. It is important to remember that a deployment manages replica sets.

Trying the command in the terminal shows three pods running:.

```
$ kubectl get pods
NAME                      READY   STATUS    RESTARTS   AGE
nginx-1-97dd4c589-dgzdj   1/1     Running   0          1m
nginx-1-97dd4c589-mn96c   1/1     Running   0          1m
nginx-1-97dd4c589-zm67c   1/1     Running   0          2h
```

One more step is to mount the newly created volume to our pods. For this, we will need to do the following steps:

1. Edit the deployment YAML file so we can add the volume mount point and the volume claim. This is followed when we deploy the pods (containers or workloads).
2. Kubernetes will automatically deploy a new container once YAML is updated and saved. Alternatively, we then redeploy the containers (you can also redeploy the entire deployment if needed).

3. We will then log in to a specific container to see if our disk was mounted and write a sample file to it.

4. Let's edit the YAML file for our already created deployment. In an ideal environment, you will have all the disks needed by your application created and mapped as part of your application deployment, so editing YAML is needed only if the application has added dependencies.

5. Get on your terminal and type:

```
$ kubectl get deployments
NAME          DESIRED   CURRENT   UP-TO-DATE   AVAILABLE   AGE
mywebapp-1    1         1         1            1           5m
```

For this exercise, I recreated my deployment and called it `mywebapp-1`.

6. Let's edit this deployment so we can map it to the volume claim we created earlier:

```
$ kubectl edit deployment mywebapp-1
```

7. This opens up my YAML for the deployment `mywebapp-1`. Scroll down to the `Spec: Containers:` section and add the following lines:

```
volumeMounts:
        - mountPath: /mnt/
name: myvol-mount
```

8. Under the `Spec:` section, map the `volumeMounts` to a volume claim:

```
volumes:
        - name: myvol-mount
persistentVolumeClaim:
claimName: myvolumeclaim
```

Notice that the `claimName` is the same claim we created earlier. Also, make sure the name in both `volumeMounts` and `volumes` is the same.

Following is what the final YAML block should look like:

```
spec:
containers:
      - image: nginx:latest
imagePullPolicy: Always
name: nginx
resources: {}
terminationMessagePath: /dev/termination-log
terminationMessagePolicy: File
volumeMounts:
      - mountPath: /mnt/
name: myvol-mount
dnsPolicy: ClusterFirst
restartPolicy: Always
schedulerName: default-scheduler
securityContext: {}
terminationGracePeriodSeconds: 30
volumes:
      - name: myvol-mount
persistentVolumeClaim:
claimName: myvolumeclaim
```

Save this in the Terminal using :wq!. Kubernetes does a YAML check and if it fails, you will see an error.

Once successful, you will see a deployment mywebapp-1 edited message.

You should see Kubernetes redeploying the containers once the YAML is saved.

Let's log in to our container to see whether the disk was mounted:

```
$ kubectl get pods
NAME                          READY    STATUS    RESTARTS   AGE
mywebapp-1-68fb69df68-4tcpp   1/1      Running   0          5m
```

We see one pod running. Let's quickly log in to this container. We should now see the disk mounted:

 In a production environment, you should never log in to the shell of the container.

```
$ kubectl exec -it mywebapp-1-68fb69df68-4tcpp -- /bin/bash
```

This let's us bash into our container:

```
root@mywebapp-1-68fb69df68-4tcpp:/# ls
bin   dev  home  lib64    mnt  proc  run   srvtmpvar
boot  etc  lib   media    opt  root  sbin  sys  usr

root@mywebapp-1-68fb69df68-4tcpp:/# df -h
Filesystem       Size  Used Avail Use% Mounted on
overlay           95G  2.7G   92G   3% /
tmpfs            1.9G     0  1.9G   0% /dev
tmpfs            1.9G     0  1.9G   0% /sys/fs/cgroup
/dev/sdb         246G   61M  233G   1% /mnt
/dev/sda1         95G  2.7G   92G   3% /etc/hosts
shm               64M     0   64M   0% /dev/shm
tmpfs            1.9G   12K  1.9G   1%
/run/secrets/kubernetes.io/serviceaccount
tmpfs            1.9G     0  1.9G   0% /sys/firmware
```

As you can see, the volume is now mounted to the container. If this container is deleted, everything except the volume will get deleted. I stored a sample file in this volume earlier called helloWorld, let's see if it exits:

```
root@mywebapp-1-68fb69df68-4tcpp:/# ls mnt
helloWorldlost+found

root@mywebapp-1-68fb69df68-4tcpp:/# cat /mnt/helloWorld
Hello World!
```

You have now created and attached a persistent volume to your container for stateful applications!

Configuring cluster networking

Now that we have a cluster deployed with three nodes and a deployment with varying number of pods, let's look at how to expose these pods so we can access our application. Kubernetes services are exposed by using a load balancer. Load balancing allows your cluster services to be available on a single IP address. In Kubernetes, you create **internal** load balancers, which make it easier for you to expose your services between GCP applications, if needed.

For our exercise here, exposing the deployed pods to the internet is easy. If you noticed, we had deployed the `nginx` images as our workloads. Let's look at exposing this to the internet so we can access our pods:

1. Open up your workload and click on **Expose**:

2. You will see the next screen that allows you to map an external port to an internal port. This internal port is the port your application talks to in the pod. In our example, `nginx` being a web server, talks to port `80`. The default value is the same value as the port number:

3. Next, we need to select the **Service type**. A service is defined as a policy by which you access a set of pods (or a workload/deployment). Kubernetes services support TCP (default) and UDP:

   - **Cluster IP**: This exposes the service to a internal IP and choosing this option makes the service reachable from within the cluster. This is also the default service type.
   - **Node port:** This mode exposes the service at each node's IP address and a port number. You will be able to access the service by going to the node's IP address and the associated port number.

- **Load balancer:** This exposes your service externally via a load balancer and makes it accessible to the internet:

4. Let's deploy a load balancer and check whether we can access our website running on containers:

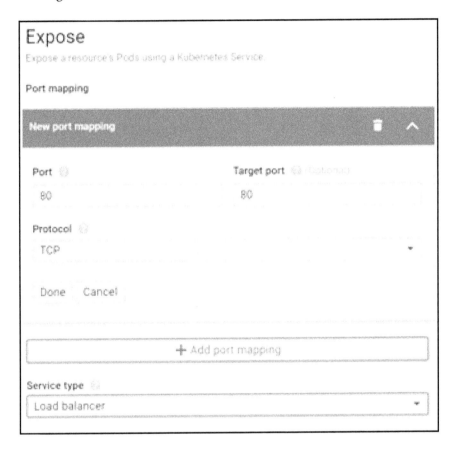

5. Click on **Expose** when you are done.

6. You will see a new service created, as shown here:

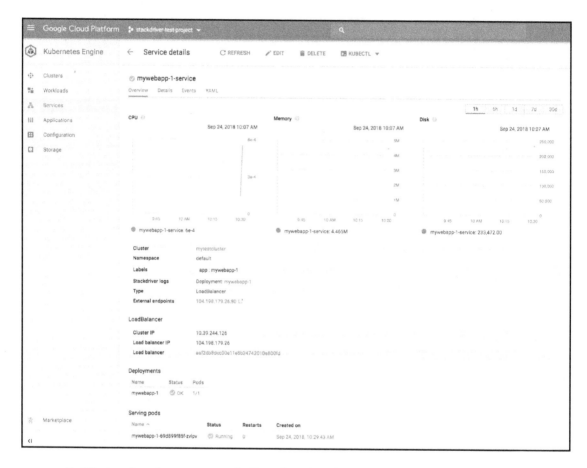

7. Notice that the status reads **Creating Service Endpoints**. This is because the Kubernetes engine is deploying an external load balancer.

8. Go to the main side menu, **Networking | Network services** and click on **Load balancing**:

9. We see a load balancer deployed with the backend having three node instances. Click on the load balancer:

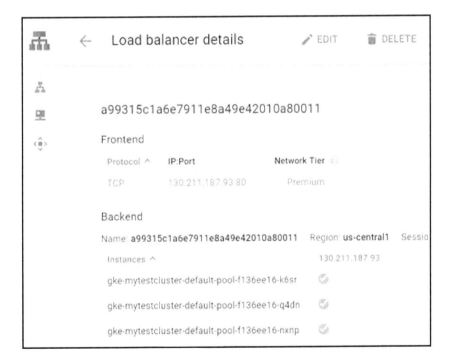

10. As you can see, the backend node instances are our three Kubernetes managed nodes from our cluster. Notice the external IP address and the port as well.

11. Open up a browser, and copy and paste the `IP:Port info` (your IP will certainly be different from what I have here). You should see the following:

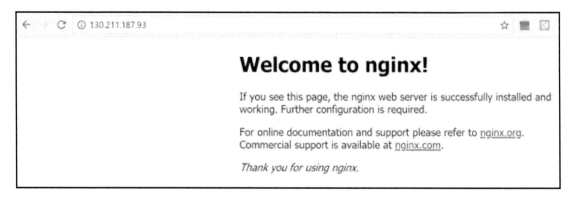

12. The load balancer receives our request and passes it on to our nodes. Kubernetes takes our request and sends it to a pod to serve that request.

13. Open up the **Services** pane in the Kubernetes engine. You should see the service deployed and mapped to the external load balancer:

14. Remember what we discussed earlier: the **cluster IP** is an internal IP on which Kubernetes pods communicate. The external load balancer passes all requests over to this cluster IP, which then routes it to the node where the pod is living. If you are wondering about firewall rules, those have already been added by the Kubernetes engine when we chose to expose the service.

15. Go to the main panel, **Networking | VPC network**. I see that a rule to allow ingress (incoming) traffic from anywhere (`0.0.0.0/0`) on port `80` is open. Let's click on it:

| k8s-fw-aaf2db8dcc00e11e8b24742010a800fd | Ingress | gke-mytestcluster-7b18b8f6-node | IP ranges: 0.0.0.0/0 | tcp:80 | Allow | 1000 | vpc-network1 |

16. You will see more specific details on the rule and also that it is enabled:

Multi-zone clusters

If you did the previous example, you must have noticed that we were deploying our cluster and its workloads in just one zone. By default, a cluster deploys all of its components (cluster master and its nodes) in a single zone. In production environments, multi-zone, or regional clusters are deployed to improve availability and to make deployments resilient to failures.

There is a difference between regional and multi-zone clusters. In a multi-zone cluster, nodes are created in multiple zones and a single cluster master is created in a specific zone. In a regional cluster, by default you create three cluster masters in three zones and nodes in multiple zones, depending on the number you need. You choose to create a multi-zone or regional clusters at the time of creation. However, you cannot downgrade or migrate once the clusters are created, so appropriate planning of your deployment is very important.

Preemptible instances

You can create your Kubernetes nodes as preemptible instances. Preemptible instances last no more than 24 hours and are deleted by GCP. These instances are priced lower than regular VM instances and offer the same configuration, making them an attractive option for running high resource consuming batch jobs. With Kubernetes, these jobs can be distributed across containers and scheduled to run on preemptible instances.

Summary

In this chapter, we looked into Kubernetes a little deeper. We started the chapter by reviewing and revisiting some core Kubernetes concepts. We then went ahead to deploy our Kubernetes cluster and also our deployment associated with it. We then created our first workload, which was an nginx container. Remember, a workload is a container and is also referred to as a pod. In advanced use cases, a pod can have more than one container. We also talked about stateful applications and deployed persistent storage to store our application state. We made this storage available to our pods and verified the deployment as well. We learned how to expose our pods or containers to the internet and therefore have access to our application on port 80, which was mapped to our nginx deployment.

There is a lot more to Kubernetes than we have discussed in this chapter, and I strongly recommend continuing your journey with Kubernetes. In Chapter 6, *Google Cloud Platform Operations*, we will learn about different GCP tools for debugging, logging, and monitoring your applications.

6
Google Cloud Platform Operations

In this chapter, we will learn about the Stackdriver suite of products that allows us to manage and debug our application. Stackdriver provides you with debug, enhanced logging, error reporting, and monitoring services for your applications. We will start with Stackdriver monitoring, which lets you monitor your applications deployed in the cloud. We will then look into its real-time logging and error reporting capabilities. We will next look at Stackdriver's **application platform management** (**APM**) capabilities by learning about its debugger, trace, and profiler features.

In this chapter, we will cover the following topics:

- Stackdriver monitoring and logging
- Stackdriver error reporting
- Stackdriver debugger
- Strackdriver profiler
- Stackdriver Trace

Stackdriver monitoring and logging

Stackdriver monitoring provides you the ability to monitor your applications deployed on GCP. Stackdriver also allows you to monitor your applications deployed in AWS as well. You can monitor your applications for performance and uptime, and all these metrics and events are collected and stored by Stackdriver. Stackdriver monitoring also generates dashboards for easy visual consumption of the data. The feature also integrates with alerting so timely alerts can be sent out for any event. Remember that monitoring and logging are closely integrated.

A better way to explore Stackdriver monitoring is to set it up for a compute engine instance. We will discuss its concepts as we go through the setup.

 I will be following Google's official documentation example here, so it will be easier for you to relate what we do here with the official guide.

Before we begin, let's review all the steps in this exercise:

1. Create a compute engine instance
2. Install an Apache HTTP server
3. Create a Stackdriver account and install agents
4. Create checks and policies
5. Create dashboards and alerts
6. Review logs

As with every other exercise we have done before, let's begin by creating a project first. If you don't already have one, go ahead and create a project called `stackdriver-test-project`:

```
$ gcloud projects create stackdriver-test-123 --name stackdriver-test-
project
Create in progress for
[https://cloudresourcemanager.googleapis.com/v1/projects/stackdriver-test-1
23].
Waiting for [operations/cp.7718643467432378132] to finish...done.

$ gcloud projects list
PROJECT_ID              NAME                          PROJECT_NUMBER
kubecluster-206421      KubeCluster                   944435304139
premium-bearing-206421  My First Project              766565060122
stackdriver-test-123    stackdriver-test-project      968775468325
```

 Project IDs and project numbers are unique. Your IDs and numbers will differ from what you see here.

Now that we have the project created, let's enable billing for it. Before we do that, let's make sure that we set our project to `stackdriver-test-project`:

```
$ gcloud config list
[core]
```

```
account = hidden@gmail.com
disable_usage_reporting = True
project = kubecluster-206421

$ gcloud config unset project
Unset property [core/project].
$ gcloud config list
[core]
account = hidden@gmail.com
disable_usage_reporting = True

Your active configuration is: [abcd]

$ gcloud config set project stackdriver-test-123
Updated property [core/project].

$ gcloud config list
[core]
account = hidden@gmail.com
disable_usage_reporting = True
project = stackdriver-test-123

Your active configuration is: [abcd]



$ gcloud config list
[core]
account = hidden@gmail.com
disable_usage_reporting = True
project = stackdriver-test-123

Your active configuration is: [abcd]
```

If you are not in the `gcloud` command line yet, this can be done easily using the GCP console:

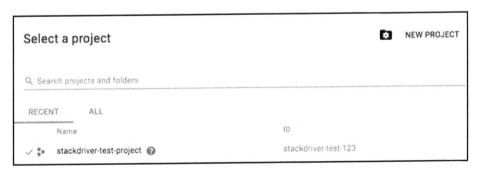

Let's enable billing for this project:

```
$ gcloud alpha billing projects link stackdriver-test-123 --billing-account
01617F-ABCSDE-AA20F0
billingAccountName: billingAccounts/01617F-B8843D-AA20F0
billingEnabled: true
name: projects/stackdriver-test-123/billingInfo
projectId: stackdriver-test-123
```

We can now create our compute engine instance in our new project. We will use the console going forward to keep things simple. If `gcloud` seems exciting, hang in there as we visit `gcloud` in Chapter 9, *Google Cloud Platform Tools*:

1. Go to your main side tab | **Compute Engine** | **VM Instances**.
2. Click **Create** after initialization is complete.
3. We will call our machine `small-http-stack` and will create it with the minimum requirements. Choose to **Allow HTTP traffic** and **Allow HTTPS traffic**:

4. Click **Create** when done. Once deployed, click on the **Connect** option and open **SSH** in your preferred method:

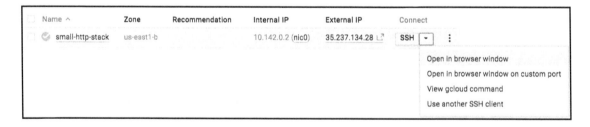

Once in, run the following commands:

```
~$ sudo apt-get install apache2 php7.0
```

This installs an `apache2` http server and a PHP on the machine. Let's make sure the service is up and running:

```
~$ sudo /etc/init.d/apache2 status
● apache2.service - The Apache HTTP Server
Loaded: loaded (/lib/systemd/system/apache2.service; enabled;
vendor preset: enabled)
Active: active (running) since Sun 2018-06-17 19:33:58 UTC;
7min ago
Main PID: 8265 (apache2)
Tasks: 6 (limit: 4915)
CGroup: /system.slice/apache2.service
├─8265 /usr/sbin/apache2 -k start
├─8267 /usr/sbin/apache2 -k start
├─8268 /usr/sbin/apache2 -k start
├─8269 /usr/sbin/apache2 -k start
├─8270 /usr/sbin/apache2 -k start
└─8271 /usr/sbin/apache2 -k start
Jun 17 19:33:57 small-http-stack systemd[1]: Stopped The Apache
HTTP Server.
Jun 17 19:33:57 small-http-stack systemd[1]: Starting The
Apache HTTP Server...
Jun 17 19:33:58 small-http-stack systemd[1]: Started The Apache
HTTP Server.
```

Some lines were ellipsized; use -l to show in full.

5. Open up a browser, and go to the IP address of your machine:

Apache2 Debian Default Page

It works!

This is the default welcome page used to test the correct operation of the Apache2 server after installation on Debian systems. If you can read this page, it means that the Apache HTTP server installed at this site is working properly. You should **replace this file** (located at /var/www/html/index.html) before continuing to operate your HTTP server.

If you are a normal user of this web site and don't know what this page is about, this probably means that the site is currently unavailable due to maintenance. If the problem persists, please contact the site's administrator.

Configuration Overview

Debian's Apache2 default configuration is different from the upstream default configuration, and split into several files optimized for interaction with Debian tools. The configuration system is **fully documented in /usr/share/doc/apache2/README.Debian.gz**. Refer to this for the full documentation. Documentation for the web server itself can be found by accessing the **manual** if the apache2-doc package was installed on this server.

The configuration layout for an Apache2 web server installation on Debian systems is as follows:

```
/etc/apache2/
|-- apache2.conf
```

6. Now that we have a functioning HTTP server deployed, let's head over to Stackdriver to set up monitoring.
7. Go to the left browsing tab | **Stackdriver** | and click on **Monitoring**.

Before we begin, Stackdriver will require us to create an account. Stackdriver accounts hold monitoring configurations for GCP projects. They also hold monitoring information for AWS accounts as well, if configured to do so. Projects are associated with a specific Stackdriver account for it to monitor those resources that are part of the project. While a Stackdriver account is necessary for monitoring purposes, logging does not require a Stackdriver account.

To enable monitoring, you first set up a Stackdriver account and then add your GCP projects and/or your AWS accounts to it. If you have a large number of projects, you can always move GCP projects between Stackdriver accounts or merge two Stackdriver accounts together. Remember that a Stackdriver account can contain up to 100 GCP projects and each project can only be monitored by one Stackdriver account.

When you create a Stackdriver account, it automatically creates additional projects that host all the dashboards and metrics, and also allow it to connect to AWS. The project that you wish to monitor using this Stackdriver account will be **in addition** to these additional projects that a Stackdriver account creates. To better explain this, let's look at the following diagram:

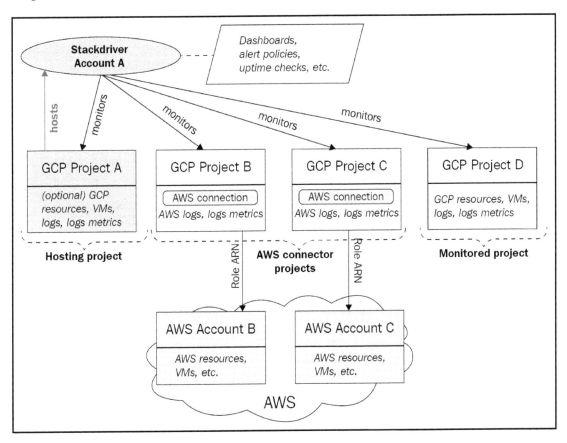

You can see that **Stackdriver Account A** manages two GCP projects, **Project A** and **Project D**, and also two AWS accounts that are managed via two GCP projects, **Project B** and **Project C**. Each project here is given a role. The dotted lines represent these roles:

- **Hosting project**: This project holds the monitoring configurations for the account, which include dashboards, uptime checks, and policies. It is advised not to deploy any of your machines or instances in this hosting project.
- **AWS connector project**: When you add an AWS account to a Stackdriver account, it automatically creates the AWS connector project for you. Your AWS instances, such as EC2, must send their logs and metrics to this connector project for Stackdriver to pick them up. If you put any GCP resources in this project, those will not be monitored by Stackdriver.
- **Monitored project**: All instances that you deploy for production will need to go into this monitored project. Any new projects that you want to be monitored by this Stackdriver account will automatically be called **monitored projects**.

Let's go back to our dashboard and create a Stackdriver account for our project:

1. Select your `stackdriver-test-project` and click **Create account**. Select the projects to add to this account. Because this is a lab, I am going to be using the `stackdriver-test-project` as a Stackdriver hosting account and also as an account where my compute engine lives:

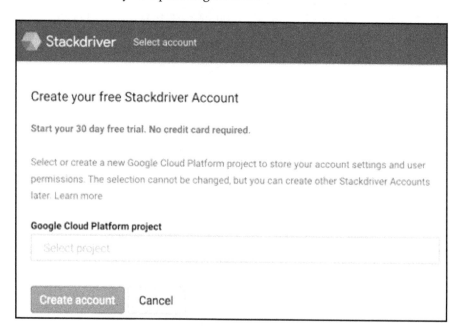

2. Click **Continue**. We will **Skip AWS Setup**, but it is good to glance at it and note what information is needed to set up your AWS account:

3. Next, we will need to install the monitoring and logging agents on your instance. You can simply copy these commands and run them on your VM by logging in to it:

4. Click **Continue** when done.

5. Select **No reports** and click **Continue**:

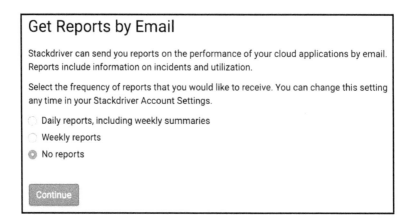

6. Next, you will see Stackdriver gathers all information and metrics through a **Launch Monitoring** button. Clicking that will give you the landing page for your project:

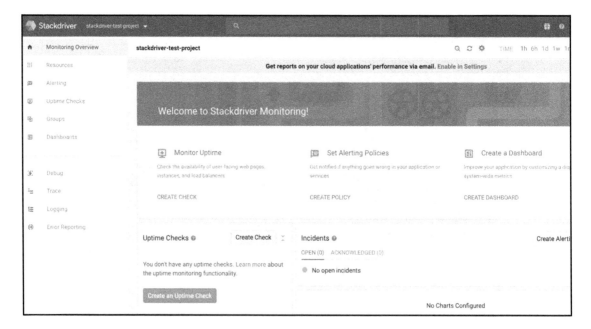

7. Let's create a simple dashboard. Click on **CREATE DASHBOARD**:

8. Type in the name for this dashboard; we will call it CPU Perf:

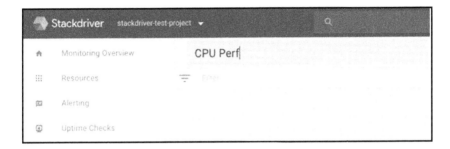

9. On the right side, click on **Add Chart**. Name the chart CPU Usage and click in the box to select a **Resource type**:

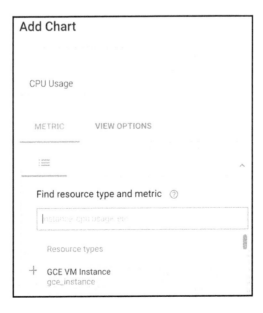

10. Select **gce_instance**, and in the **Metric**, scroll down to select **CPU usage**:

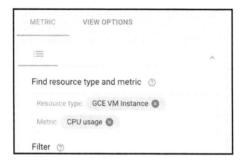

11. You should already see the right side of the graph populated. Click **Save** when done. You will see the chart added to our dashboard:

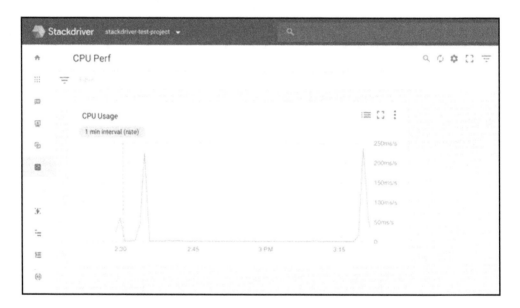

Let's create some CPU load:

1. In our GCP compute instance we created, run this command:

   ```
   ~$ sudo apt-get install stress
   ```

2. This will install `stress`, which allows you to create load on your CPU with a set `timeout`. Once installed, run the following command and watch the dashboard:

   ```
   ~$ sudo stress --cpu 2 --timeout 120
   ```

3. Now refresh your dashboard, and you will see a spike in CPU usage:

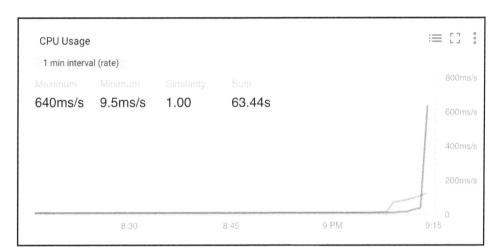

You can also create uptime checks, alerting policies, and custom metrics, using Stackdriver monitoring. Uptime checks help to monitor and alert, if the application or the check fails. You can configure the uptime checks from the main landing page or on the side-bar tab.

Logging

Let's look at the logging feature for Stackdriver. If you recall from the earlier section, we installed the logging agent as part of our Stackdriver account setup. Click on **Logging** on the side bar tab to open a new window. You can select different resources, which include **GCE Project**, a **GCE Firewall Rule**, or even a **GCE VM Instance**:

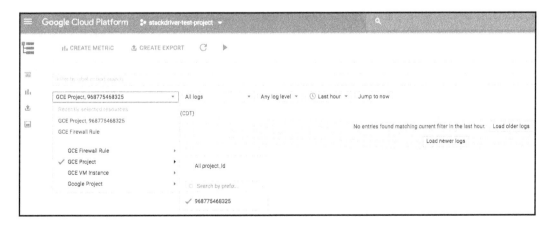

Click on **Load older logs** to review these logs:

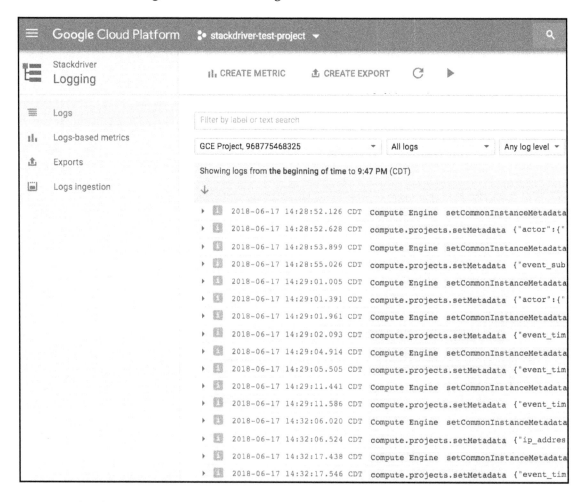

You can also filter using the **Any log level** option, or using the time frame:

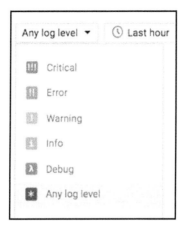

Let's select our virtual machine instance and review its logs:

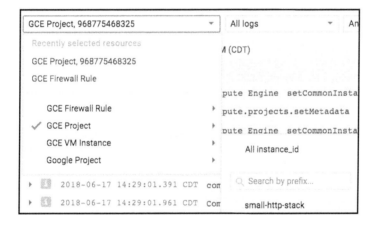

I intentionally stopped the Apache2 web server and noticed these new logs at the bottom:

```
▸    2018-06-17 21:51:48.000 CDT Jun 18 02:51:48 small-http-stack systemd[1]: Stopping The Apache HTTP Server...
▸    2018-06-17 21:51:48.000 CDT Jun 18 02:51:48 small-http-stack systemd[1]: Stopped The Apache HTTP Server.
▸    2018-06-17 21:51:48.896 CDT [Mon Jun 18 02:51:48.896209 2018] [mpm_prefork:notice] [pid 8265] AH00169: caught SIGTERM, shutting down
```

Let's start the Apache2 web server and see whether the logs reflect this event. Click on the **Jump to now** button on top of the page to load the latest logs:

```
▸    2018-06-17 21:53:00.000 CDT Jun 18 02:53:00 small-http-stack systemd[1]: Starting The Apache HTTP Server...
▸    2018-06-17 21:53:00.000 CDT Jun 18 02:53:00 small-http-stack systemd[1]: Started The Apache HTTP Server.
▸    2018-06-17 21:53:00.724 CDT [Mon Jun 18 02:53:00.724031 2018] [mpm_prefork:notice] [pid 17383] AH00163: Apache/2.4.25 (Debian) config
▸    2018-06-17 21:53:00.726 CDT [Mon Jun 18 02:53:00.726690 2018] [core:notice] [pid 17383] AH00094: Command line: '/usr/sbin/apache2'
```

Now we'd like the logs to auto-populate. For this to happen, enable **Log streaming**:

This will auto-populate any new logs created by system events on your machine. One last thing to note is that you can directly view logs from the dashboard charts by clicking the **View Logs** option:

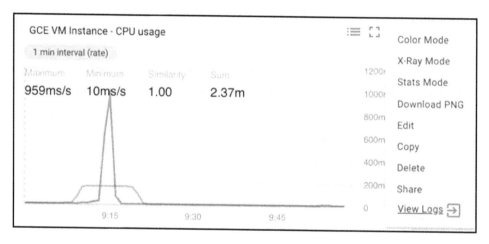

Stackdriver error reporting

Stackdriver error reporting aggregates and displays errors in your cloud services. Stackdriver error reporting works with Google App Engine and Google Cloud Functions, with beta versions available for Google Compute Engine and AWS EC2. All application errors can be captured by Stackdriver error reporting by logging application errors to Stackdriver logging:

Let's learn more about Stackdriver error reporting by deploying a simple app on Google App Engine. We will then introduce and capture an error in the app.

In your main GCP console, go to your side bar menu and click on **App Engine** | **Dashboard**. Make sure you are in your desired project and billing is enabled. I am using the `Stackdriver-test-project` that we created earlier.

You will see a quick start guide on the right. Let's follow that guide and deploy our `Hello World` app in a Python platform:

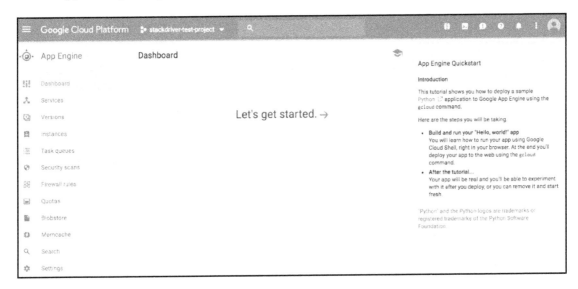

Click **Continue** for the quick-start guide:

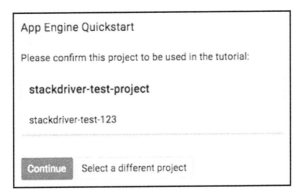

Click **Continue**. Follow the instructions and clone the sample code in your cloudshell console. Make sure you remember or copy these commands; we will be introducing failures in the app once it's deployed using the same commands.

If you followed the quick-start guide, you will have an app deployed that runs on Python and returns `Hello World` when you access its URL:

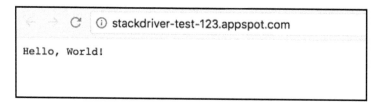

You will see the app we deployed listed in the **Services** tab under the **App Engine** pane:

Now that we have a running app, lets introduce an error. Open a new cloudshell, git clone the sample web app, and edit the **main.py** file. Change the import statement to `import webapples`.

Run this command:

```
gcloud app deploy app.yaml --project stackdriver-test-123
```

 The `gcloud` command can be run from either CloudShell (that pops up in the GCP web console) or on your command line of your machine if GCP cloud SDK is installed. We will learn more about these two tools in greater detail in the upcoming chapters.

You will now see a new version of your app deployed:

You will also see two versions of the app:

Let's click on the latest version, which is currently serving traffic:

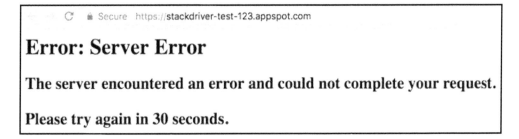

Now that we have introduced an error, let's visit **Error Reporting** in the **STACKDRIVER** menu:

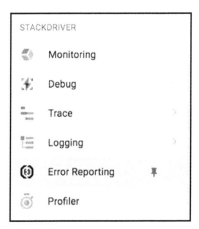

You will see an error shown in the **Error** list:

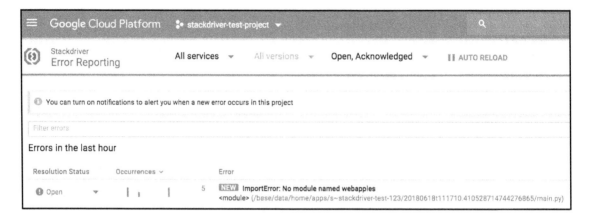

Click on **AUTO RELOAD**; this causes the error list to refresh every five seconds:

Click on the error:

You will see occurrences, which shows how many times this error happened. The more times you access the web app's URL, the more occurrences happen. Errors are grouped and deduplicated, so instead of seeing five errors of the same kind, you will see 500 Internal Server Error grouped as shown before.

Right below this dashboard, click on **Recent samples**, and you will see all the available details here. You will also see the line number and the file where the error happened:

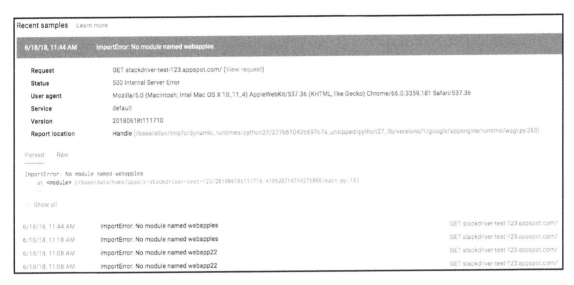

Explore the UI a bit more and understand how you can easily identify errors in your deployed apps. Continue to run this faulty app, as we will try to fix it in the next section, using the Stackdriver debugger.

Stackdriver debugger

The Stackdriver debugger allows you to inspect and analyze the state of your applications in real time without having to stop the application. With the debugger, you will be able to capture the call stack and variables without slowing down the application; this is particularly helpful if you want to debug or trace your code and understand its behavior. Stackdriver does this by capturing the application state by means of debug snapshots, which add less than 10 ms to the latency:

Debugger supports a variety of platforms:

Language	App engine		Compute engine	Kubernetes engine
	Standard	Flexible		
Java	Yes	Yes	Yes	Yes
Python	Yes	Yes	Yes	Yes
Go	-	-	Yes(Beta)	Yes(Beta)
Node.js	Yes[1]	Yes(Beta)	Yes(Beta)	Yes(Beta)
Ruby	-	Yes(Beta)	Yes(Beta)	Yes(Beta)
PHP	No	Yes(Alpha)	Yes(Alpha)	Yes(Alpha)
.NET Core	-	Yes(Alpha)	No	Yes(Alpha)

Let's explore the debugger with the `Hello World` app we deployed earlier. We will use the version that works. If you deleted the app, simply follow the earlier process and redeploy the app.

Navigate to the **Debug** page in the side-bar tab:

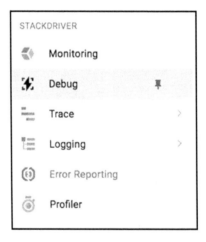

You will see the **Stackdriver Debug** dashboard with our app. The Stackdriver debugger uses source context information to display the correct version of the source code here. This source code information is captured in the `source-context.json` file. When we deployed our Python app, a `source-context.json` file was generated and uploaded with our application. The Stackdriver debugger uses this file to load the correct version of the source code that is in production.

If you have custom source code, you can choose to load it into the debugger by clicking the dropdown on the left and selecting **Add source code**:

You will see a host of options to load your source code. This code is not uploaded to the GCP servers but instead uses HTML5 APIs and is loaded in the browser. This is only supported on Google Chrome currently:

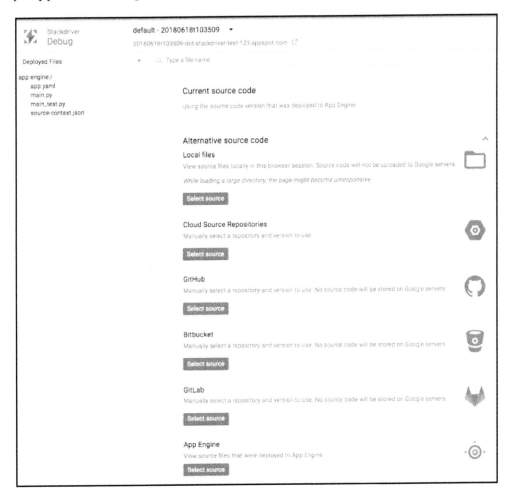

Let's go back and load our application:

You can filter between apps by selecting the **App** in the drop-down menu. I selected the app that works without any errors:

Let's take a debug snapshot for our application. A debug snapshot captures the local variables and call stack at a specific line location in your code. Let's take a snapshot on line 20 where an error was intentionally added to our code in the main.py file.

Click on the line number. You will see a blue marker:

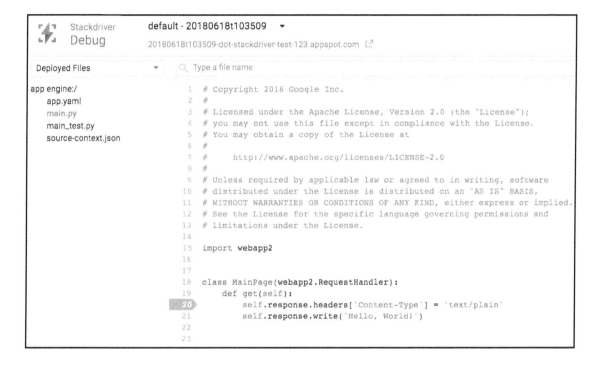

On the right side, you will see the status change to `Waiting for snapshot to hit.`
`The running application will not stop.`:

If you are not sure how many snapshots were taken, locate **Snapshot History** at the bottom of the page:

You will see that the debugger is ready to take a snapshot at line 15 of the main.py file:

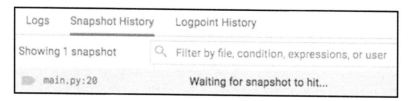

We will now send a request to our app to capture the variables and the call stack at that specific line. Simply click on your web app URL above the page:

Once the browser loads the page and sends the request to your app, the debugger captures the stack. You will see the following in your console:

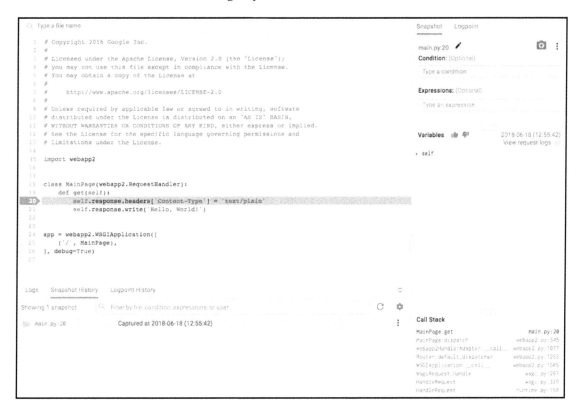

The **Call Stack** panel shows all the results and values of local variables captured at that point in the code and at that point in time. You can even browse through the variables captured:

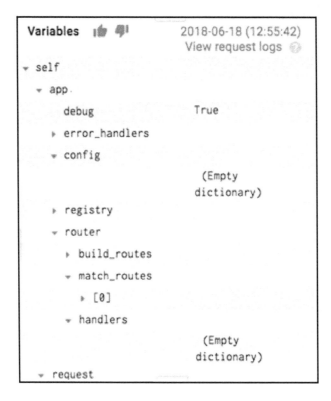

Let's take this a step further and add a debug logpoint. A logpoint enables you to inject logging into your running app without the need to stop it or restart it. Select the **Logpoint** tab right next to the **Snapshot** tab:

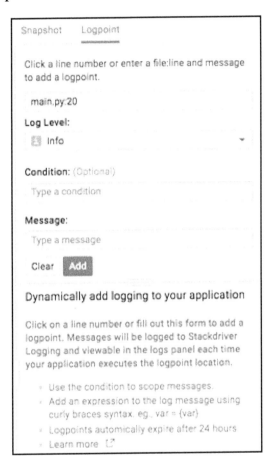

Let's add a simple logpoint **Message**:

Once you have finished, click **Apply**:

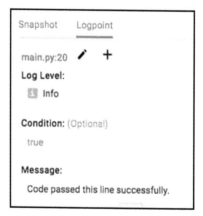

You will see that the `logpoint` is created. Make note that this `logpoint` is only valid for 24 hours. In the **Logpoint History** tab, you will see the `logpoint` created:

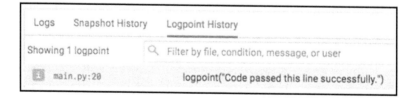

Most noticeable is the `logpoint` added to the code:

```
18    class MainPage(webapp2.RequestHandler):
19        def get(self):
              logpoint("Code passed this line successfully.")
              self.response.headers['Content-Type'] = 'text/plain'
21            self.response.write('Hello, World!')
```

Let's go back to the web app URL and initiate a request. Select the **Logs** panel at the bottom of the page to see your logpoint trigger:

```
Logs    Snapshot History    Logpoint History

Q   Search by text

                                        Showing logs older than 2018-06-18 (13:11:15.086) — Load more

▸   2018-06-18 (13:11:15.086)  LOGPOINT: Code passed this line successfully.
```

Stackdriver profiler

The Stackdriver profiler helps gather CPU usage and memory allocation information from your applications. This is different than Stackdriver monitoring, because with the Stackdriver profiler, you can tie the CPU usage and memory allocation attributes back to your application's source code. This helps you identify parts of your application that consume the most resources and also allows you to check the performance of your code:

Let's go over a hands-on exercise to explore and understand the Stackdriver profiler. In this lab, we will download a sample Go program and run it with the profiler enabled. We will then explore and use the profiler interface to capture data.

Let's log into our GCP console and select a project. Go to the **Stackdriver | Profiler** tab on the side bar and click on it:

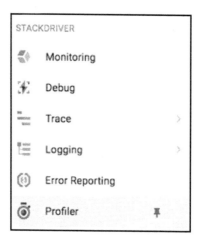

You will see the **Stackdriver Profiler** main page:

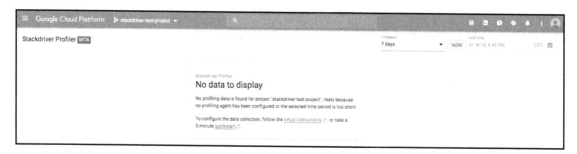

The previous action also enables the Stackdriver profiler API.

Next, we open a `cloudshell` and download the sample Go program from GitHub:

```
@cloudshell:~ (stackdriver-test-123)$ go get -u
github.com/GoogleCloudPlatform/golang-samples/profiler/...
```

Next, use `ls` to list the directory and access the sample code for the Stackdriver profiler:

```
cd ~/gopath/src/github.com/GoogleCloudPlatform/golang-
samples/profiler/profiler_quickstart
```

The file is called `main.go`. The program is written to create a CPU-intensive workload to provide data to the profiler. The program is configured to use the Stackdriver profiler, which collects profiling data from the program and saves it periodically. You will see only two messages as the program runs that indicate the progress:

```
successfully created profile CPU
start uploading profile
```

It is important to note that you need to configure your code with the Stackdriver profiler to be able to collect profiling data. You can profile code written in Go, Java, Node.js, and code written outside GCP. Across these platforms, only certain types of profiling are available. The following table illustrates this:

Profile type	Go	Java	Node.js
CPU	Y	Y	
Heap	Y		Y
Contention	Y		
Threads	Y		
Wall		Y	Y

Let's look into each of these profile types:

- The CPU time for a function describes how long it took to execute the code for a function. This only includes the CPU processing time and not the CPU wait time.
- Heap profiling helps you find potential memory usage inefficiencies in your programs.
- Contention allows you to profile a mutex contention for Go. This allows you to determine the amount of time spent waiting for mutexes and the frequency at which contention occurs.
- Threads allows you to profile thread usage for Go and captures information on goroutines and Go concurrency mechanisms.
- Wall or wall-clock time is a measure of the time elapsed between entering and exiting a function.

You can use profiling agents on Linux in the compute engine, Kubernetes engine, and app engine flexible environments. You will need to add code additions, depending on the language you use, to profile those specific profile types.

Code additions are out of scope for this book. For now, just remember that code additions allow your profiler to run and collect data. This data is then analyzed using the profiler interface.

In the cloudshell that you have open, type in the following:

```
go run main.go
```

As mentioned earlier, the program is designed to increase the load on the CPU as it runs, and the Stackdriver profiler collects and saves the data periodically.

Your output will show the following:

You will see the **Stackdriver Profiler** dashboard change:

If you don't see any updates, click on **NOW** on the right side to update it with the latest profiled data:

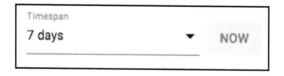

Notice that over five profiles were updated in my demo:

100%, averaged over 5 profiles

Here are these updates being logged in the console:

```
2018/06/19 13:30:21 successfully created profile CPU
2018/06/19 13:30:31 start uploading profile
2018/06/19 13:31:00 successfully created profile CPU
2018/06/19 13:31:10 start uploading profile
2018/06/19 13:32:01 successfully created profile CPU
2018/06/19 13:32:12 start uploading profile
2018/06/19 13:32:52 successfully created profile CPU
2018/06/19 13:33:02 start uploading profile
2018/06/19 13:33:54 successfully created profile CPU
2018/06/19 13:34:05 start uploading profile
```

Let's explore the profiler interface. The interface offers a control area for selecting the data to visualize and a flame graph representation of the selected data. You can use the top controls for selecting a specific time range, so you can examine the data for that time frame.

Let's see the following options available to us in the profiler dashboard:

Service allows you to switch between different applications that are being profiled. Profile type lets you choose the kind of profile data to display; in this case CPU. Zone names allow you to restrict your data to a particular zone and versions allow you to restrict profiled data from specific versions of your application. The **Add profile data filter** allows you to filter out or refine how the graph displays data.

Let's explore the colorful flame graph:

The top frame (gray colored) represents the entire program. This frame always shows 100% of the resource consumption. Below the top frame, each of these frames represents each function and its size (measured horizontally) shows the proportion of resource consumption that function is responsible for. The main green function is the Go runtime.main function. The orange frame is the main routine of the sample program. The orange busy loop and load frames are routines called from the main function of the program.

If you look closely, the four functions consume almost the same amount of resources. To understand where the resources are allocated, we can use the filter option to hide the call stack from the main routine.

Type in Hide stacks: main, and hit *Enter*:

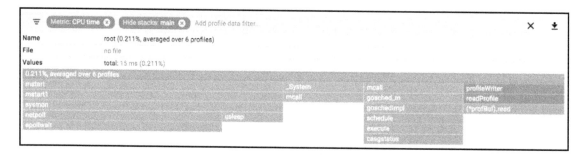

This shows all the resources consumed outside our program, and it accounts for 0.211% over the six profiles we processed.

Try deploying different applications with the sample profiler code and continue to explore the behavior of your application with this powerful tool.

Stackdriver Trace

Stackdriver Trace is a distributed tracing system that collects latency data from applications, Google App Engine, and HTTP(s) load balancers, and displays it in near-real time in the GCP console. For applications to be able to use this feature, they need to have the appropriate code in place with the Stackdriver Trace SDKs, but this is not needed if your application is being deployed in Google App Engine. Stackdriver Trace greatly enhances your understanding of how your application behaves. Things like time to handle requests and complete RPC calls can be viewed in real time using Stackdriver Trace:

Some use cases for Stackdriver Trace include the following:

- Reviewing historical latency data
- Reviewing detailed latency data, including performance insights and RPC calls
- Generating custom reports for latency data, and building comparison models for latency data

As mentioned before, Stackdriver Trace is tightly integrated with Google App Engine, so any application you deploy in the app engine can be traced using Stackdriver Trace. During runtime, app engine sends latency data to Stackdriver Trace for requests for the application URIs and for round-trip RPC calls. Stackdriver Trace does not work with Cloud SQL.

Let's explore the dashboard to understand Stackdriver Trace. On your side menu tab, go to **Stackdriver** and click on **Trace | Overview**:

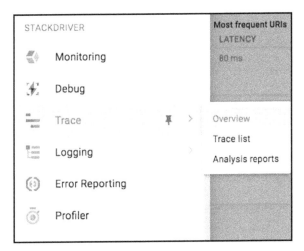

You will see an **Overview** dashboard similar to the following:

Click on **Trace list** to view recent requests to your application:

I am using the web app we deployed in the beginning of this chapter. You can see Stackdriver Trace is picking up the requests to the URI.

You can click on a specific request to get more information:

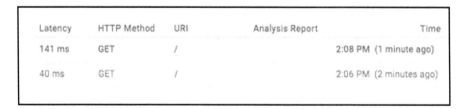

Clicking on the first request gives you the timeline for the request:

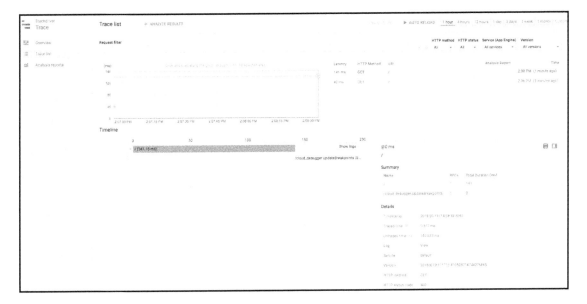

You can create an analysis report for your traced data.

Click on the **Analysis reports** option:

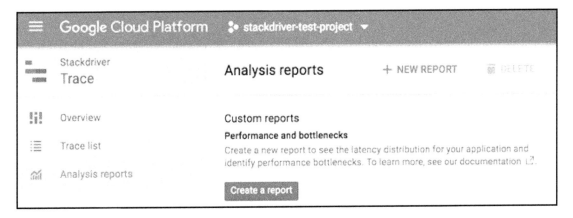

Click on **NEW REPORT** to create a new report:

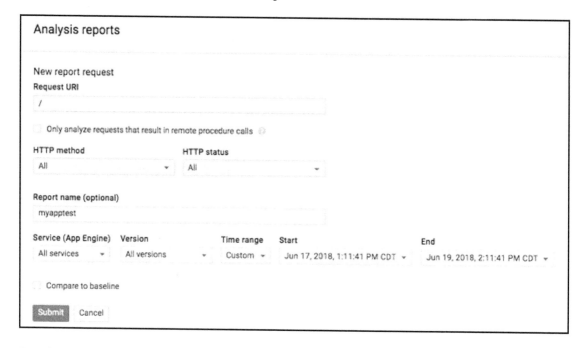

For the **Request URI**, we have a /, which indicates that this report must contain information for all requests made to the application.

If you get this message, it means that you have too few traces to create a meaningful report:

The request will not produce a useful report because it had less than 100 traces. Create a new report with a longer time range or less-restrictive filter.

Once the report is generated, you can access it by clicking on **Analysis**, and here is what a sample report will look like:

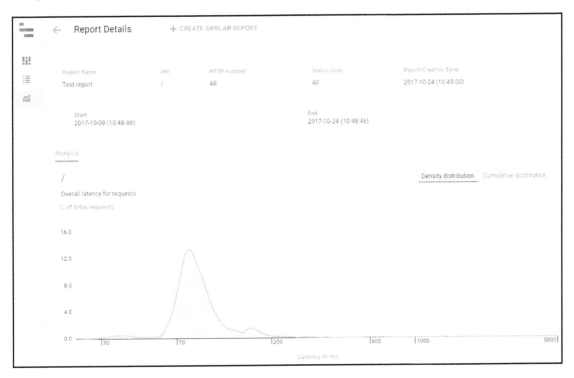

This is a powerful tool to use in your environment to better understand the behavior of your code and your application. It is important to remember that for an app that is running in a virtual machine or a container, Stackdriver Trace is not automatically enabled or traced. This is also the case for apps running in the GCP App Engine flexible environment. You will need to use libraries or the Stackdriver Trace API to send traces to the service. You can enable or set up Stackdriver Trace for platforms such as C#, Java, Go, Node.js, Ruby, and PHP.

Summary

In this chapter, we learned a lot about using GCP tools to understand the behavior of your deployed applications. We started this chapter by talking about Stackdriver monitoring and logging, which allow you to monitor and capture application logs. We got our hands dirty by deploying a web app and setting it up with monitoring and logging. We then looked at Stackdriver error reporting, which aggregates and displays errors in your cloud services. Remember that Stackdriver error reporting works with Google App engine and Google cloud functions, and beta services include GCP Compute Engine and AWS EC2. We then dug deeper into the Stackdriver APM suite, which includes Stackdriver debugger, the Stackdriver profiler, and Stackdriver Trace. These three tools combined give us a much richer understanding of how our application behaves in production environments, without having to introduce any downtime or latency.

7
Google Cloud Platform Identity and Security

In this chapter, we will learn about GCP identity and security. We begin the chapter with a brief overview of Google's infrastructure security layers and its cloud platform security. We will learn about identity access management and the **key management service** (**KMS**)—two services that are core to how you allow role-based and key-based access to your GCP environment. We will briefly look into cloud security scanner. We will also learn about security keys, which allow you to secure your account using two-step verification. In this chapter, we will cover the following:

- Infrastructure and cloud platform security
- Identity access management
- Key management service
- Cloud security scanner
- Security keys

There is a lot more to identity and security service offerings than what this chapter covers. This brief overview will help you get started with GCP's security offerings.

 Identity and access management (**IAM**) is a concept/methodology that is cloud agnostic. Every cloud provider provides a similar set of IAM capabilities.

Infrastructure and cloud platform security

Google is an internet powerhouse and has been building core services and infrastructure, and security has been imperative to Google throughout its journey. Google has security built through layers, from data center security all the way to application and information management. The following diagram gives you a good idea of this layered security approach at Google, along with the different capabilities and features at each layer:

Operational Security			
Intrusion Detection	Reducing Insider Risk	Safe Employee Devices & Credentials	Safe Software Development

Internet Communication	
Google Front End	DoS Protection

Storage Services	
Encryption at rest	Deletion of Data

User Identity	
Authentication	Login Abuse Protection

Service Deployment			
Access Management of End User Data	Encryption of Inter-Service Communication	Inter-Service Access Management	Service Identity, Integrity, Isolation

Hardware Infrastructure		
Secure Boot Stack and Machine Identity	Hardware Design and Provenance	Security of Physical Premises

The lowest layer is the hardware infrastructure security, which includes physical security, hardware security, and machine boot stack security. Google designs and fully owns and manages its data centers, and access to these data centers is highly restricted. A fun fact is that Google even uses laser-based intrusion detection systems at their physical data center locations. Google also has some co-location functions hosted at partner data centers, and Google's physical security standards extend to partner data centers as well. Google hosts thousands of servers at these data centers, and all these servers and pieces of network equipment are custom-designed by Google. Google also designs custom boards, including hardware security chips, that enhance a device's security. The security boot stack is a system built by Google where cryptographic signatures are used to validate low-level components such as BIOS, bootloader, kernel, and so on. This ensures that any system that may be compromised at that level can quickly be isolated.

As we go up the stack, we have service deployment, where Google deploys and manages services such as an app engine running either Google's or a customer's application. Although Google uses ingress and egress firewall filtering to filter traffic, it does not primarily rely on internal network segmentation for security. Google uses cryptographic authentication, which validates authorization at the app layer. Every service is associated with a service account identity, along with cryptographic credentials. The services use these credentials to validate and are only then allowed to make calls to other services. Inter-service access management allows an owner of a service to specify which services are allowed to talk to his service, and this further tightens the access security for your service. Google also provides encryption for all these inter-service calls on the networks. Even if the network is compromised, the messages will mean nothing because of the encryption in place. The access management of end user data allows a service to create an end user permissions ticket, which is used to access another service. This allows a narrow and defined set of access for what the user is trying to do, rather than give full access to the service.

The third layer from the stack allows services such as authentication and login abuse protection. Google offers a range of authentication techniques, which include setting up two-factor authentication to enhance security. Login abuse protection provides best practices that can be enforced on different types of logins, and also remediation and protection methods if logins are compromised.

For storage services, Google provides an Encryption at Rest capability which uses a central KMS to encrypt data, and also allows us to automatically rotate the encryption keys. When a customer wants to delete some data, Google begins that process by first marking that data as **scheduled for deletion**. This protects the data from accidental deletion and allows for a quick recovery. After a set period of time, set by a service-specific policy, Google permanently deletes the data. If the hard drive needs to be decommissioned, the data is purged in a multi-step process. If the data cannot be properly cleaned, then the hard drive is shredded and destroyed.

While all the layers discussed until now deal with services and infrastructure, with the internet communications layer, we enter the zone that isolates the Google environment from the public internet. Google's frontend service or GFE allows a service to register to it to get public accessibility. GFE is sort of a gatekeeper that ensures that all TLS communications are terminated using proper certificates. Any service that is published externally uses GFE as a smart reverse-proxy frontend. Google also provides multitier and multilayer **denial-of-service** (**DoS**) protection. The DoS service further reduces any attacks on a service running behind GFE. Lastly, Google offers a central identity service, which allows end users to log in and access GCP services.

The last layer of operational security is focused on the different aspects of Google that allow for the secure operation of infrastructure. As part of safe software development, Google provides libraries that prevent developers from using certain classes that can introduce software bugs. Google also uses manual security reviews, from quick triages to in-depth design and implementation reviews. To keep employee devices and credentials safe and to deter phishing, Google has replaced **one-time password** (**OTP**) devices with mandatory use of **Universal 2nd Factor** (**U2F**)-compatible security keys. Google also logs employee access to end user information through low-level infrastructure hooks, and these logs are actively monitored and investigated.

Identity and access management

IAM allows you to define users and roles and help control user access to GCP resources. GCP offers Cloud IAM, which allows you to grant granular access to users for specific GCP resources based on the least privilege security principle.

Cloud IAM is made up of members to whom access is granted. The following diagram shows the different kinds of member types and also roles, which are collections of permissions. When a member is authenticated and makes a request, Cloud IAM uses roles to assess whether that member is allowed to perform an operation on a resource:

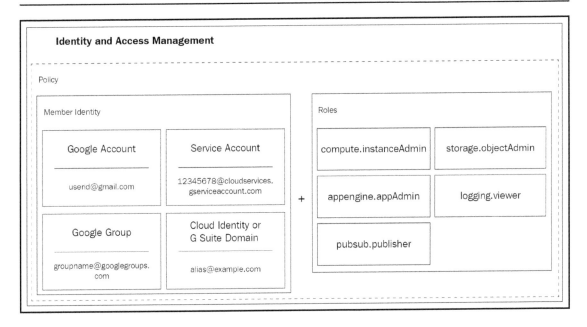

Let's briefly talk about different types of member accounts:

- **Google Account**: Any person who interacts with GCP over `https://accounts.google.com/ServiceLogin/signinchooser?service=mailpassive=truerm=false continue=https%3A%2F%2Fmail.google.com%2Fmail%2Fss=1scc=1ltmpl=default ltmplcache=2emr=1osid=1flowName=GlifWebSignInflowEntry=ServiceLogin` or custom domain account is represented by a Google account. This person can be a developer, an administrator, or an end user with access to GCP.
- **Service Account**: A service account is an account that is associated with an application. Code that runs on your GCP account runs under a service account. Multiple service accounts can be created and associated to different parts of your application. Service accounts help create granular access and permissions.
- **Google Group**: A Google group is a collection of Google accounts and service accounts. Google groups makes it easier to apply an access policy to a collection of users. Groups also make it easy to add and remove members.

- **G Suite Domain**: Google offers organizations a G Suite Account, which offers email, calendar, docs, drive, and other enterprise services. A G Suite domain represents a virtual group of all Google accounts created in an organization's G Suite account. If your organization's name is XYZ, then G Suite domains typically represent your domain and every user created in this domain will get a new Google account inside this virtual group. For example, a user's email address will be `username@xyz.com`. G Suite domains are primarily for grouping and permission management, and are not used to establish identity.
- **Cloud Identity Domain**: The primary difference between a Cloud Identity Domain and a G Suite domain is that all users in the Cloud Identity Domain do not have access to G Suite applications and features.

Let's briefly describe the roles and permissions involved in the authorization process:

- **Roles**: A role is a collection of permissions that determine what operations are allowed on any resource. Roles are granted to users, and all permissions that role contains are applied to that user. You cannot assign permissions to a user. Permissions are represented in the form of `<service>.<resource>.<verb>`, for example, `compute.instances.delete`. Remember that a resource here is a GCP resource such as projects, compute engine instances, cloud storage buckets, and so on.

  GCP offers **primitive roles** such as owner, editor, and viewer roles. There are also **predefined roles** that give finer-grained access. You can also create **custom roles** that allow you to create custom-defined roles for your organizational needs.

- **IAM policy**: An IAM policy is a collection of statements that define the type of access a user gets. A policy is assigned to a resource and is used to govern access to that resource. An IAM policy can be set to any level in a resource hierarchy. You can set the policy at the organization level, the folder level, the project level, or at the resource level. Policies are inherited from parents so if you set a policy at the organization level, all the projects will inherit that policy, which in turn is inherited by all resources in those projects.

Let's explore the IAM page using the GCP console and familiarize ourselves with it:

1. In the GCP Console, you will find the **IAM & admin** section on the left-hand side of the screen:

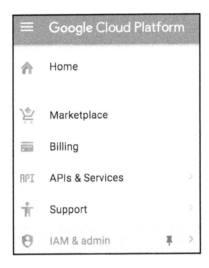

2. Click on **IAM.** You will see a list of members with the roles assigned to them:

3. Click on **ROLES** to see the roles that are currently assigned to members. The members here are Google accounts and service accounts that were created when we accessed different services across GCP:

4. To add a team member, simply click **ADD**, enter the team member account, and assign it a role:

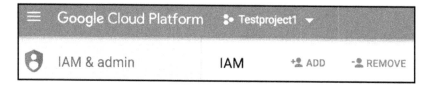

The account name has to be either a Google account email, a Google group, a service account, or a G Suite domain:

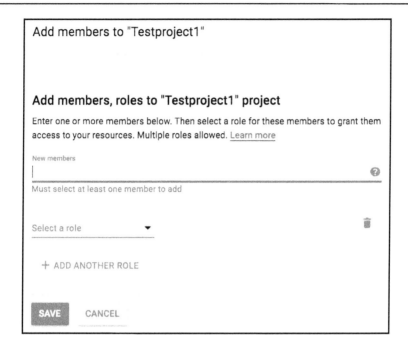

5. Next, click on the **Select a role** dropdown and pick a role. These are predefined roles, but you can create custom roles by clicking the **Roles** tab on the left-hand navigation tab. Remember, you can assign more than one role, but the most restrictive role takes precedence:

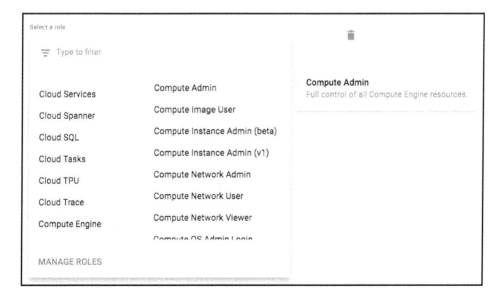

Key management service

Cloud KMS is a hosted KMS that lets you manage your encryption keys in the cloud. You can create/generate, rotate, use, and destroy AES256 encryption keys just like you would in your on-premises environments. You can also use the cloud KMS REST API to encrypt and decrypt data. Before we explore Cloud KMS, we need to understand the object hierarchy structure. Let's briefly go over the object hierarchy and then explore Cloud KMS on the GCP console.

To enhance access control management, Cloud KMS stores keys in a hierarchical structure. There are different levels in the hierarchical structure:

1. **Project**: Like every other GCP resource, Cloud KMS resources belong to a project. All primitive IAM roles that are applied to a project also apply to your KMS.
2. **Location**: You can create Cloud KMS resources in multiple locations within a project. These locations are where Cloud KMS handles requests and also stores the keys. However, when you create your keys in a global location, Cloud KMS resources are available from multiple data centers.
3. **Key ring**: An application can have multiple keys, which will be used for different resources. A key ring is a grouping of keys for easier management purposes. A key ring belongs to a project and is always placed in a specific location. All the keys in a key ring inherit permissions from the key ring that contains them. You can now easily alter permissions to all keys at the key ring level rather than having to do it at the per-key level.
4. **Key**: A key is an object representing a cryptographic key. All keys are **256-bit Advanced Encryption Standard** (**AES-256**) keys and using the same key, version to encrypt the same plain text will result in two different cipher texts. As a security measure, you can only use the key to encrypt or decrypt but can never view, copy, or export. As you create new keys, the key's "material"—the bits used to encrypt data—can change over time as new key versions are created. As a key version changes, the key changes as well. You use a key to encrypt your data without worrying about the version. Cloud KMS can easily identify which key version was used and can decrypt the data upon request; the key version data is stored in the encrypted data (cipher text). Key versions have states: enabled, disabled, scheduled for destruction, or destroyed. A key at any point in time will have a primary version, which is used by Cloud KMS to encrypt data. As you create a new key version and make that version the primary version, you can rotate keys. After creating a new key version and marking it as the primary version, the older versions do not get deleted or destroyed, and are still available for decrypting data:

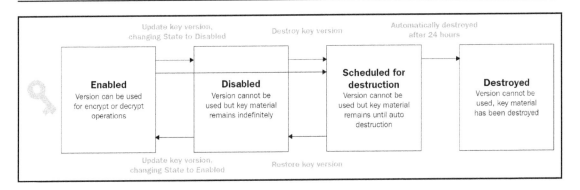

It is important to regularly rotate keys by creating new versions. This way, all data will be encrypted by a variety of keys and the threat of exposure is greatly reduced. You can provide a rotation schedule, which includes a rotation period—the time between key rotations—and a next rotation time—when the key rotation can happen.

It is important to remember that key rings and key resources cannot be deleted. Key versions cannot be deleted either, but the key material (the key bits that encrypt data) can be destroyed. Key rings and keys do not have any quota limitations or billable costs, so they can be used and created without any impact on performance or price.

Let's go ahead and create some cryptographic keys using the GCP Console.

Open up your GCP console and log in. On the left-hand tab, go to **Security** and click on **Cryptographic keys**:

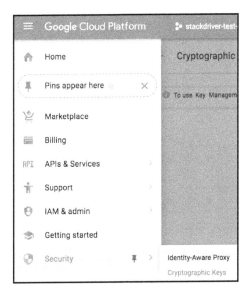

You will see a notification that shows that you need to enable the KMS API before you start creating the keys:

> ⓘ To use Key Management you must enable Google Cloud Key Management Service (KMS) API, and setup billing. Learn more

Click **Setup** on the right-hand side of the screen to enable the API and set up billing. Once the API is enabled, click on the **Create key ring** button in the center of the screen. Remember, a key ring is a grouping of keys that is created at the **Project** level. All keys in a key ring remain in a specific location:

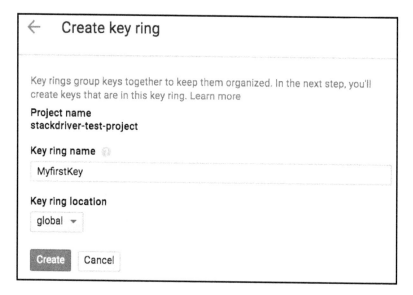

Click **Create** to begin creating a key in this key ring:

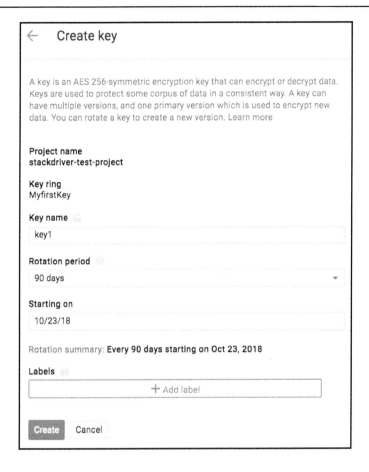

Click **Create**.

You will now see your key available. Click on the key name to see its version number and also options to rotate it:

When you click on **ROTATE**, you will see the following:

Rotate key key1

When you rotate a key, this immediately happens:
- A new version will be created and made the primary version.
- New data will be encrypted with the new version.

Older versions can be used to decrypt data. Data encrypted using older key versions will remain so unless explicitly re-encrypted.

CANCEL   ROTATE

When you rotate the keys, you will see a new version created and the state set to **Enabled & Primary**. The older version state is **Enabled**. Now that you have the key, you can encrypt and decrypt any file using this key.

Cloud security scanner

Cloud security scanner is built to identify vulnerabilities in your Google App Engine applications. The scanner crawls through your application and can attempt to try multiple user inputs in order to detect vulnerabilities. The scanner can detect a range of vulnerabilities, such as XSS, flash injection, mixed content, clear text passwords, and use of JavaScript libraries.

Cloud security scanner can only be used with the Google App Engine standard environment and compute engine. You cannot use the security scanner with a Google App Engine flexible environment. When requested, cloud security scanner does not start immediately but is queued by GCP to scan the app at a later time when the load is low. It is advisable to run the security scanner in a lab environment. Running cloud security scanner in a production environment can create undesirable data. For example, if you run a blog, cloud security scanner can post test comments of random text to check whether public posts are vulnerable. The security scanner does not delete this text, leaving them on your website for everyone to see.

To run a scan, log in to your GCP portal and go to the **App Engine** tab:

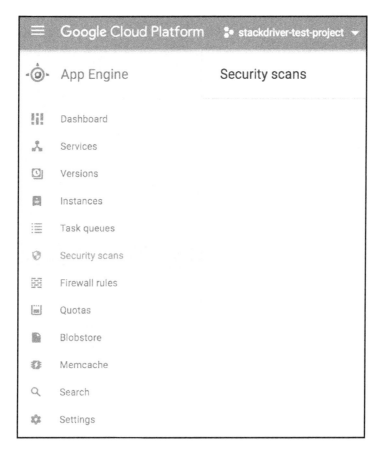

You will need to enable its API before you can use it. Click on **Enable API** in the center of the screen. Once enabled, you can click on **Create scan**:

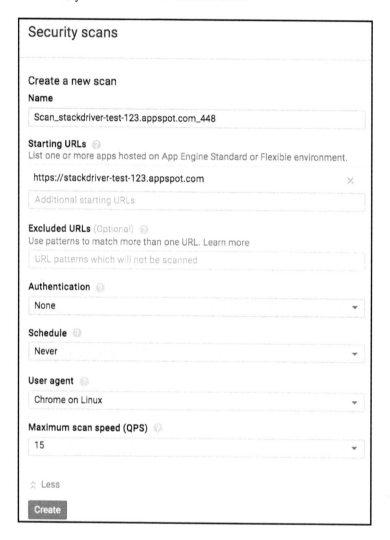

You will need to have an app running; here, the security scanner has picked up my app. You can mention additional URLs if needed. Click **Create** when done:

Click **Run scan** to begin scanning this app.

The scan results are shown in the following screenshot:

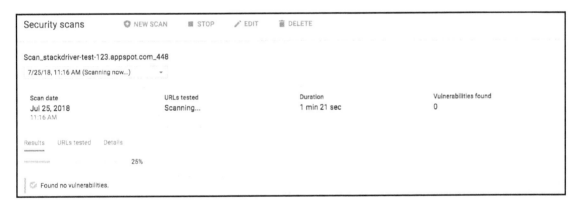

Data loss prevention

The **data loss prevention** (**DLP**) API provides a programmatic way to classify 90+ types of data. For example, if you have a spreadsheet with financial and/or personal information, parsing this data with the DLP API masks and hides all this sensitive information. With this API, you can easily classify and redact sensitive data. At the time of this writing, only contextual and image-based data can be classified and redacted using the DLP API.

Instead of having to stream all data into the API, the DLP API allows you to do storage classification scans that allow contextual data to be scanned in cloud storage or cloud datastore.

Security keys

Security keys are a type of two-step verification process to secure your Google account and protect it from any unauthorized access. Some two-step verification methods supported/provided by Google are text message, Google Authenticator, and security keys. The text message and Google Authenticator methods require you to have your mobile phone. Google sends a OTP and Google Authenticator is a downloadable app that can generate OTP tokens on your mobile. Hackers are known to use a phishing attack to attempt to steal your password and OTP.

Security keys are not susceptible to phishing attacks. Security keys are small USB hardware dongles that generate a cryptographic signature when touched. This signature is used in lieu of an OTP. Being USB devices, a security key requires a computer with a USB device. Security keys are powered by the FIDO U2F open authentication standard, which means you can buy this key off the shelf and configure it to be used with GCP.

To register a security key, you will have to go into your Google account settings. Once registered, every time you log in with your username and password, you will be prompted for the security key. Insert the security key and tap it to be able to log in.

Summary

We have covered many topics in this chapter, but there is a lot more to security and identity services than this chapter covers. We started this chapter learning about Google's security layers, followed by identity access management and the KMS. We also briefly learned about cloud security scanner, which scans for vulnerabilities in your app deployed in the Google App Engine standard environment. We also briefly looked into the DLP API and security keys.

Google Cloud Platform Billing

8

We have spent time learning and understanding the different aspects of the Google cloud platform. In this chapter, we will provide a high-level overview of GCP billing. We begin this chapter with some billing concepts and learn to manage billing. We will briefly discuss how to analyze a billing cycle, set up a budget, and also set up billing alerts. This will be a short chapter with a focus on some basic billing features.

In this chapter, we will cover the following:

- Billing concepts
- Managing billing
- Analyzing a billing account
- Setting up a budget and alerts

Billing concepts

GCP offers flexible ways to set up and manage billing for your resources. A billing account is how a user pays for the resources being consumed. A billing account is associated with a method of payment and access is established using Cloud IAM roles. For a resource to be deployed in a project, the project has to be associated with a billing account. More than one project can be associated with a billing account.

GCP offers two types of billing accounts:

- **Self-served**: This type of billing account serves well for small deployments where the payment method is a debit/credit card or by using a bank account. You will be billed automatically and these types of accounts can be created at any time. Typically, a demo environment uses such accounts.
- **Invoiced**: This type of account is where payments can be made by check and invoices are generated and mailed to the user. Invoiced billing requires you apply for **eligibility** by contacting Google support.

Costs incurred by a Google account are charged in two ways, monthly billing and threshold billing. In monthly billing, costs are charged on a monthly cycle. In threshold billing, you will be billed when your account has accrued a specific amount. For example, you can set the threshold billing to bill you when your bill reaches $1,000. Remember that if the threshold cost is reached within 30 days, then you will be billed immediately. If the threshold is not reached, you will be billed in 30 days.

Picking the right billing method depends on your use case. For predictable costs, monthly billing cycle is ideal.

You can also create **sub-accounts**, which are linked to the master billing account. Projects can be linked to these sub-accounts, which can then be used to track the costs. Sub-accounts help in generating custom invoices for resellers or for charge-back purposes:

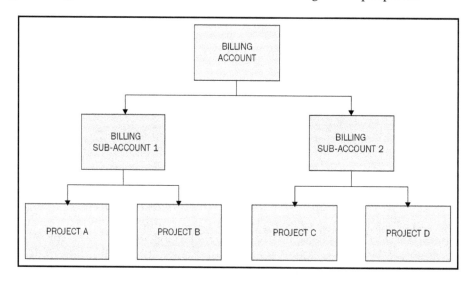

For all intents and purposes, a sub-account behaves the same as a master billing account. You can also use the **cloud billing API** to create sub-accounts on demand, associate them with proper roles, and link projects to them.

Managing billing

Managing billing is easy with GCP. Let's explore this by logging in to our GCP console and clicking on the dashboard. You will see the **Billing** card on the right-hand side of the screen:

In the left-hand navigation pane, click on **Billing**:

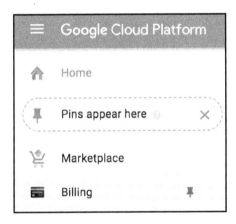

You will see the **Billing** dashboard and an overview of your account:

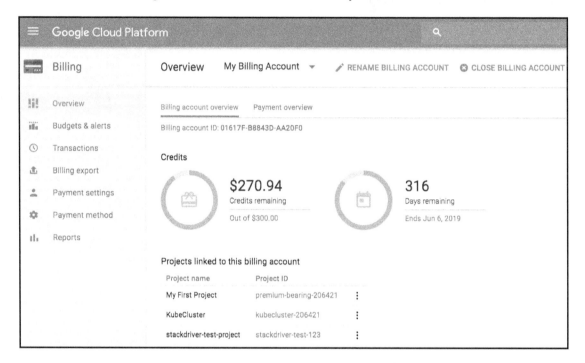

In the preceding illustration, you can see the that this GCP account has $270.94 worth of credits remaining out of the $300 initially applied. You also see the days remaining before these credits expire. The list of projects linked to this account is also listed giving you a snapshot of the different consumers. Notice the **Budgets & alerts** on the left where you can create a custom budget and also create alerts.

There are a variety of options here, including the ability to rename the billing account or close it. Closing the billing account will require you to pay all dues. Click on the **Payment overview** tab to review your payment methods. You can even manage payment methods, such as adding a new credit card or a bank account.

At the top of the page, beside the **Overview** button, click on the dropdown to select **ALL BILLING ACCOUNTS**. You can use this option to view all accounts, open and closed. You can even re-enable a closed billing account:

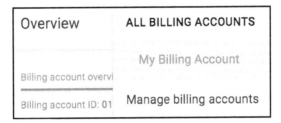

Analyzing a billing account

On your GCP console **Billing** dashboard, click on **Payment settings**:

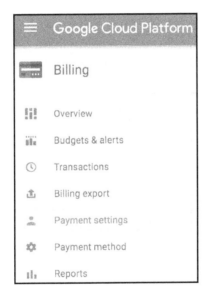

You will see your payment account ID and also note your payment option; it is set to **Automatic payments**.

Click on **Billing export**. Google allows you to export your billing as a **BigQuery dataset** or as a file export. You can use these features to further analyze your billing and resource consumption activity to further reduce costs. You will need a BigQuery dataset before you can export your billing data. For the file export, you will need a cloud storage bucket where the data will be stored.

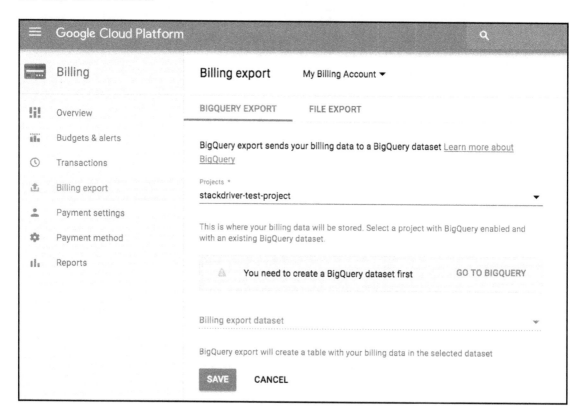

You can import this data into a **Billing** Dashboard using Google's data studio suite. The following is a sample output based on some test data:

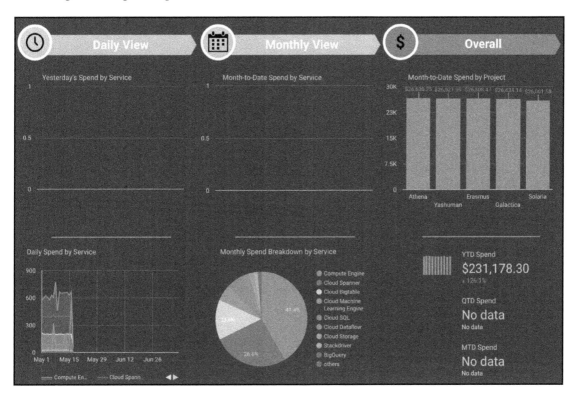

Setting up a budget

You can control your costs and plan better by setting up a budget. Setting up a budget helps you track your expenses and manage them efficiently. Budgets can be created and applied either to a billing account or specifically to a project. All resources created in that project are then accounted for in that budget. You can also create alerts to ensure that you are not exceeding your budget.

In the **Billing** page of your GCP console, click on **Budgets & alerts** on the left-hand side of the pane. Click on **Create budget**:

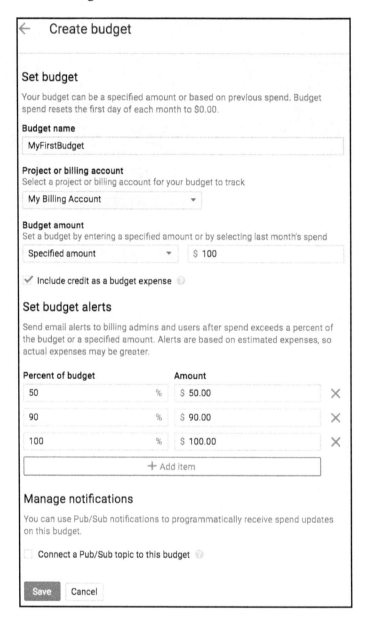

As you can see, creating a budget is fairly easy. You add multiple alert percentages that help you keep track of your usage. You can even connect a pub/sub topic to programmatically receive updates. This can be useful if you have an internal billing system that manages your corporate billing:

Because we marked **Include credit as a budget expense,** you will see the credit usage also shown as part of the budget. If you want to create more alerts, simply click on the budget name and add or remove alerts.

Summary

This was a relatively short chapter that focused on GCP billing. GCP offers flexible billing options and also the ability to dashboard your GCP spending. We started the chapter by covering some basic GCP billing concepts. We discussed managing and analyzing billing. We also set up a budget and alerts that help us manage our bills efficiently without overspending. The next chapter talks about Google cloud platform tools such as deployment manager, cloud SDKs and GCP marketplace.

Google Cloud Platform Tools

9

In this chapter, we will go over a high-level overview of GCP tools. We will begin by briefly discussing GCP Deployment Manager and learn how easy it is to deploy your applications using the Deployment Manager. We will also learn more about `GCP marketplace` and deploy a marketplace application. GCP has a powerful set of SDKs and APIs and we will discuss these briefly. We will also look into `cloud shell`, something we have been using earlier in our console.

The following topics will be covered in this chapter:

- Deployment Manager
- GCP marketplace
- GCP Cloud SDKs
- Cloud API
- Cloud shell
- Summary

Deployment Manager

Deployment Manager allows you to create templates of your resources or applications that can easily be deployed ondemand. This allows for automation and management of GCP resources using YAML-based configuration files. For example, if your company has an application that is often deployed, you can create a Deployment Manager template for it and run it every time the application needs to be deployed.

Let's look at some basic concepts of Deployment Manager:

- **Configuration:** A configuration describes all the resources that are part of a single deployment. The resources can be anything—GCP compute instances, app engine instances, or storage buckets. The configuration file is written in YAML and consists of each resource type along with its properties. Every resource must have a name, a type, and its properties.
- **Template:** Templates are parts of configuration files that have been abstracted into individual blocks. For example, as part of every app deployment, if you create four compute engine instances and three BigQuery data tables, then this process can be made part of a template and included in different configuration files. A template file is written in either Python or Jinja 2.
- **Types:** Every resource in Deployment Manager has a **type** associated with it. A type can be a single API resource known as a base type or a set of resources known as a composite type.
- **Manifest:** A manifest is a read-only object that contains the original configuration you provided to the Deployment Manager. Every time the deployment manager is updated, a new manifest file is generated.

Let's explore Deployment Manager in the GCP Console:

1. Log in to your GCP console and click on **Deployment Manager** which is listed under **TOOLS**:

2. We will deploy a single VM configuration using **Deployment Manager**. If you haven't already, download and install the cloud SDK.
3. Set the project ID:

```
$ gcloud config set project stackdriver-test-project
Updated property [core/project].
```

Replace the `stackdriver-test-project` with your own project name.

4. Next, we create a configuration file in YAML. A configuration file starts with the `resources` string. On your machine, create a folder and create a file called `1-vm.yaml`. In this YAML file, type the following code. Be mindful of the spaces and remember not to use tabs for spacing.

5. In the following file, we mention the name of our virtual machine and the instance type. We also have the zone on which this gets deployed. This will override any default zone that is part of your `gcloud config`. We have also mentioned the disks and the network settings for this deployment:

```
resources:
- name: my-vm
    type: compute.v1.instance
    properties:
      zone: us-central1-f
      machineType:
https://www.googleapis.com/compute/v1/projects/myproject/zones/
us-central1-f/machineTypes/f1-micro
      disks:
      - deviceName: boot
        type: PERSISTENT
        boot: true
        autoDelete: true
        initializeParams:
          sourceImage:
https://www.googleapis.com/compute/v1/projects/debian-cloud/glo
bal/images/family/debian-9
      networkInterfaces:
      - network:
https://www.googleapis.com/compute/v1/projects/myproject/global
/networks/vpc-network1
        accessConfigs:
        - name: External NAT
          type: ONE_TO_ONE_NAT
```

 Replace `myproject` with the name of your project.

6. Save changes to the file. To deploy this configuration, run this command:

```
$ gcloud deployment-manager deployments create deployment-1-vm
--config 1-vm.yaml
```

7. If the `deployment manager` API is not enabled, you will see the following message:

```
API [deploymentmanager.googleapis.com] not enabled on
project[414958921078]. Would you like to enable and retry (this
will take a few minutes)? (Y/N)?
```

8. Type in `Y` to continue:

```
Waiting
for
 create operation
-
1482984765292
-
146afeb8d00f1
-
b826f0e7
-
b792463
...
done
.
Create
    operation operation
-
1482984765292
-
146afeb8d00f1
-
b826f0e7
-
b792463 completed successfully
.
NAME            TYPE                STATE      ERRORS  INTENT
my
-
vm   compute
.
v1
.
instance  COMPLETED
[]
```

You have successfully created a new deployment.

It is important to remember that deleting a deployment will also delete all resources deployed by that deployment. To delete this deployment, enter:
`$ gcloud deployment-manager deployments delete 1-vmdeploy.`

GCP marketplace

Google allows you access to its vast marketplace where you can readily and easily access different applications and software packages. Let's deploy a simple WordPress application from the marketplace:

1. On your GCP Console, go to **TOOLS** and **Deployment Manager**.
2. Click on **DEPLOY MARKETPLACE SOLUTION**:

3. You will see a list of different applications that are available:

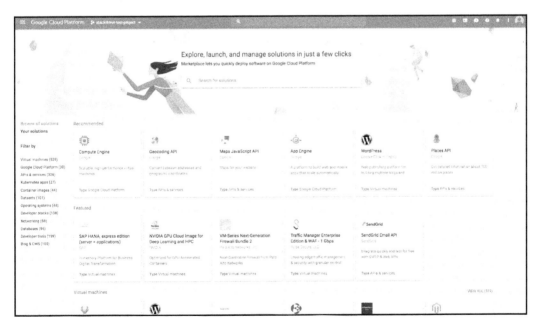

List of different applications

2. Click on **WordPress** and click on **Launch on Compute Engine**:

3. Click **Deploy** when ready. Make sure you enter an **Administrator Email**.
4. You will now see the application being deployed in **Deployment Manager**. You will see a step-by-step deployment of the application:

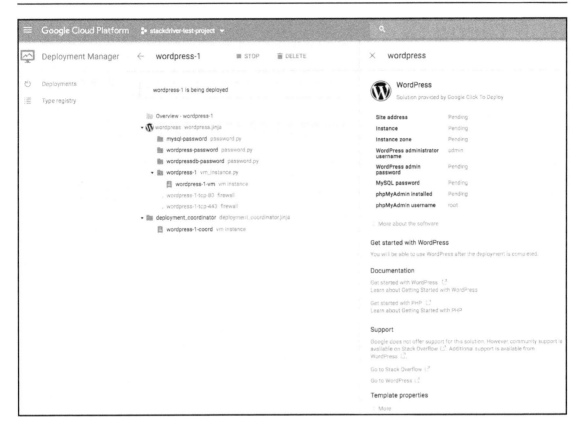

5. Under **Deployments**, you will see the following:

You have successfully deployed a WordPress (blogging) application from the GCP marketplace. Deleting the deployment will delete all components of the application, including resetting the network firewall configurations. The deletion process is handy, especially when you have deployed applications consuming hundreds of resources.

GCP Cloud SDK

Throughout this book, we have been using the cloud SDK in some shape or form. Cloud SDK provides a set of tools to manage GCP resources. Recall the use of the command gcloud which is just one of the command line tools that cloud SDK offers. Cloud SDK has other command line tools as well, such as gsutil and bq. Cloud SDK can be installed on various platforms such as Linux, Debian/Ubuntu, macOS, RedHat, and Windows.

Cloud SDK is made up of components. Components are installable parts of the SDK, such as command-line tools or packages that contain dependencies for tools in SDK. Components also allow you to access tools that are in Alpha or Beta testing phases. When you install the cloud SDK, the following components are installed: gcloud, bq, gsutil, and core. The gcloud tool gives you the ability to interact with GCP using commands in the terminal. This is ideal for day-to-day users and even for scripting. The bq tool is a BigQuery command-line toolkit, and gsutil is a tool set for Cloud Storage operations. The core tool is an SDK library used by SDK tools.

You can install the Cloud SDK by going to https://cloud.google.com/sdk/ and downloading the version that is appropriate for your machine. You need to make sure you have Python 2.7.x. Once downloaded, unpack the archive and run the command, gcloud init to initialize the SDK. The gcloud init command is the first command that you run to configure your account. Once this is done, all gcloud commands will be executed within the realms of that GCP account and within the confines of a project:

```
$ gcloud init
Welcome! This command will take you through the configuration of gcloud.

Settings from your current configuration [trsingh] are:
core:
  account                    gmail.com
  disable_usage_reporting: 'True'
  project: stackdriver-test-123

Pick configuration to use:
 [1] Re-initialize this configuration [trsingh] with new settings
 [2] Create a new configuration
 [3] Switch to and re-initialize existing configuration: [default]
Please enter your numeric choice:  
```

You can review your active configuration properties by typing gcloud config list:

```
$ gcloud config list
[core]
account =              @gmail.com
disable_usage_reporting = True

Your active configuration is: [default]
$
```

In the preceding screenshot, note that this configuration is marked as **default**. You can create multiple configurations and name them, and switch between them as per your requirement. Typically, while operating multiple projects, this multi-configuration capability will be helpful. Use the gcloud config configurations create [name] command to create a named configuration. You can also list all available configurations using the gcloud config configurations list command.

To view the components installed, type gcloud components list:

```
$ gcloud components list

Your current Cloud SDK version is: 213.0.0
The latest available version is: 213.0.0

┌─────────────────────────────────────────────────────────────────────────────────────────┐
│                                       Components                                          │
├───────────────┬──────────────────────────────────────────┬────────────────────────┬────────────┤
│    Status     │                   Name                   │           ID           │    Size    │
├───────────────┼──────────────────────────────────────────┼────────────────────────┼────────────┤
│ Not Installed │ App Engine Go Extensions                 │ app-engine-go          │ 152.8 MiB  │
│ Not Installed │ Cloud Bigtable Command Line Tool         │ cbt                    │   4.8 MiB  │
│ Not Installed │ Cloud Bigtable Emulator                  │ bigtable               │   4.3 MiB  │
│ Not Installed │ Cloud Datalab Command Line Tool          │ datalab                │   < 1 MiB  │
│ Not Installed │ Cloud Datastore Emulator                 │ cloud-datastore-emulator │ 17.4 MiB │
│ Not Installed │ Cloud Datastore Emulator (Legacy)        │ gcd-emulator           │  38.1 MiB  │
│ Not Installed │ Cloud Pub/Sub Emulator                   │ pubsub-emulator        │  33.4 MiB  │
│ Not Installed │ Cloud SQL Proxy                          │ cloud_sql_proxy        │   2.5 MiB  │
│ Not Installed │ Emulator Reverse Proxy                   │ emulator-reverse-proxy │  14.5 MiB  │
│ Not Installed │ Google Cloud Build Local Builder         │ cloud-build-local      │   4.4 MiB  │
│ Not Installed │ Google Container Local Builder           │ container-builder-local │  4.4 MiB  │
│ Not Installed │ Google Container Registry's Docker credential helper │ docker-credential-gcr │ 1.8 MiB │
│ Not Installed │ gcloud Beta Commands                     │ beta                   │   < 1 MiB  │
│ Not Installed │ gcloud app Java Extensions               │ app-engine-java        │ 118.6 MiB  │
│ Not Installed │ gcloud app PHP Extensions                │ app-engine-php         │  21.9 MiB  │
│ Not Installed │ gcloud app Python Extensions             │ app-engine-python      │   6.2 MiB  │
│ Not Installed │ gcloud app Python Extensions (Extra Libraries) │ app-engine-python-extras │ 28.5 MiB │
│ Installed     │ BigQuery Command Line Tool               │ bq                     │   < 1 MiB  │
│ Installed     │ Cloud SDK Core Libraries                 │ core                   │   8.3 MiB  │
│ Installed     │ Cloud Storage Command Line Tool          │ gsutil                 │   3.6 MiB  │
│ Installed     │ gcloud Alpha Commands                    │ alpha                  │   < 1 MiB  │
│ Installed     │ kubectl                                  │ kubectl                │   < 1 MiB  │
└───────────────┴──────────────────────────────────────────┴────────────────────────┴────────────┘

To install or remove components at your current SDK version [213.0.0], run:
  $ gcloud components install COMPONENT_ID
  $ gcloud components remove COMPONENT_ID

To update your SDK installation to the latest version [213.0.0], run:
  $ gcloud components update
```

You can always use `gcloud components install <component name>` to install a new component that is not part of the default.

For example, `gcloud components install kubectl` installs the Kubernetes components.

To update your `Cloud SDK` version, simply run `gcloud components update` to update your tools.

Cloud API

Google's Cloud API provides libraries to programmatically access and manage your GCP environment. You can access your GCP environment directly from your server applications, using the client libraries which are supported on multiple languages. Cloud APIs are JSON REST and also provide an RPC interface. This RPC interface allows clients to make API calls using gRPC.

You can use the API dashboard which provides the project's API usage, traffic bandwidth, error rates, and so on. We looked at the API dashboard earlier in this book.

Before using an API, it needs to be enabled by using the console **APIs & Services** | **Library**:

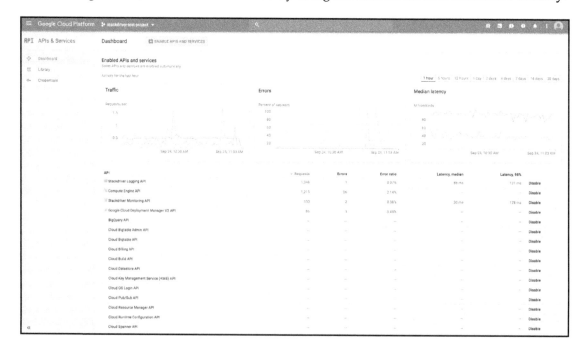

Select a project and click on the specific API that you want to enable for that project. For example, you may want to only enable the compute engine API for your project. In the preceding screenshot, you will see different services with their enabled APIs. You can click on the **Disable** button to disable them individually. Selectively enabling an API, enhances your deployment security and prevents unauthorized access. You can click on **ENABLE APIS AND SERVICES** at the of the page to select and enable specific APIs.

Cloud API also provides client libraries that make it easier for you to consume GCP services using your desired programming language. You can choose between the **Google Cloud Client Libraries** and the **Google API Client Libraries**. Not all GCP services offer the cloud client libraries. **Google API Client Libraries** provide access to API's REST interface only and do not support gRPC.

To enable the compute engine API, click on **ENABLE APIs AND SERVICES** and select **Compute Engine API**:

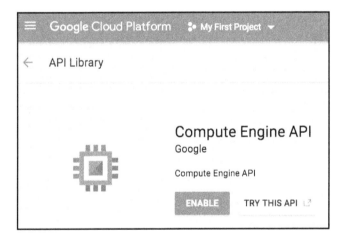

Click **ENABLE** to enable the API. Enabling the API is not always done manually. When you deploy or use a service for the first time, the API is automatically enabled before the deployment happens. Enabling an API takes a minute or two to happen, as Google prepares the services in the backend.

Once the API is enabled, the dashboard gets updated, as shown here:

Cloud shell

Cloud shell is an interactive shell environment that allows you to manage your GCP resources programmatically, without having to install the Google Cloud SDK. Cloud shell comes readily configured with the `gcloud` command so you can easily manage your GCP resources. When you click on the cloud shell icon, GCP will deploy a temporary compute engine, `g1-small` virtual machine, with 5 GB of persistent disk storage. You will also see a command-line access to that instance pop up in the web browser.

These cloud shell virtual machine instances are provisioned per user and on a per-session basis. This instance terminates after one hour of inactivity or when you exit your session. The persistent disk, mounted as a `$HOME` directory, remains even after the cloud shell instance is destroyed. This `$HOME` directory is private to you.

Once this instance is fully deployed and initialized, you will see the shell prompt. This instance comes fully configured with the Google Cloud SDK and is able to manage your environment and multiple projects as needed.

Cloud shell also offers a cloud editor which can be used to browse file directories as well as view/edit files. The code editor is another way to enhance your usage of the environment using cloud shell. Other features of cloud shell include a boost mode that temporarily upgrades your cloud shell instance to `n1-standard-1` virtual machine. This is handy when you need more CPU and memory to run scripts when needed.

Go to your web console and in the upper right-hand top corner, click on the icon to Activate Cloud Shell:

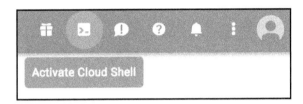

You will see the bottom of the screen pop up with a connecting status, as shown next. It can take up to 25–40 seconds for the cloud shell to be active, if there isn't an active session or a cloud shell virtual machine instance. The cloud shell instance is already configured to be used with your GCP account so there is typically no need to run the `gcloud init` command to initialize. It is also important to remember that you will not be charged for the cloud shell virtual machine and its resources. Cloud shell is free for customers:

You can also click on the pop-out icon if you prefer to use cloud shell in its own web window. On the right-hand side of this frame, click on the Launch code editor BETA icon to start the code editor:

Launching the code editor opens a new window with the editor as shown here:

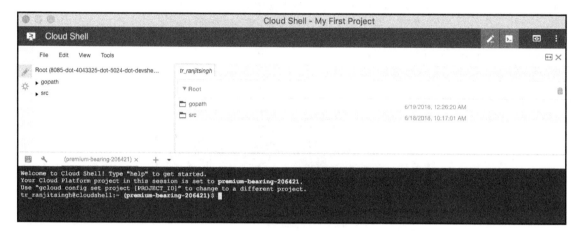

Cloud shell also comes with the ability to preview your application. Click on the Web preview icon as shown here. This icon is also accessible in the regular cloud shell frame without the need to launch the code editor:

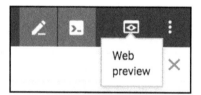

Upon clicking the web preview, you will see the option to pick the port on which your web application can be accessible for preview in the GCP console. The ports need to be within the range of 8080 and 8084. Web preview is great because it only allows you to preview your application behavior in real time without exposing it to the outside world:

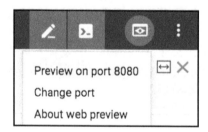

Cloud shell is a very powerful tool that can make a developer's life easy. It also makes it easy to manage your GCP environment without the need to install SDK tools. In fact, even before downloading the SDK toolkit, I spent a considerable amount of time experimenting using cloud shell which made things easy.

Summary

In this chapter, we learned about Deployment Manager and created a YAML configuration file. We used the Deployment Manager to deploy a virtual machine using the YAML file we created. We also learned about the GCP marketplace and deployed a blogging application from the marketplace. The chapter only touches on some basic concepts and it is highly recommended that you continue your learning on Deployment Manager uses and concepts. We also looked into GCP Cloud SDK's and cloud API—two ways to interact with GCP programmatically. We briefly looked into cloud shell which is a powerful, easy to access tool that is readily available.

Other Books You May Enjoy

If you enjoyed this book, you may be interested in these other books by Packt:

Google Cloud Platform for Architects
Vitthal Srinivasan, Janani Ravi, Judy Raj

ISBN: 978-1-78883-430-8

- Set up GCP account and utilize GCP services using the cloud shell, web console, and client APIs
- Harness the power of App Engine, Compute Engine, Containers on the Kubernetes Engine, and Cloud Functions
- Pick the right managed service for your data needs, choosing intelligently between Datastore, BigTable, and BigQuery
- Migrate existing Hadoop, Spark, and Pig workloads with minimal disruption to your existing data infrastructure, by using Dataproc intelligently
- Derive insights about the health, performance, and availability of cloud-powered applications with the help of monitoring, logging, and diagnostic tools in Stackdriver

Google Cloud Platform for Developers
Ted Hunter, Steven Porter

ISBN: 978-1-78883-767-5

- Understand the various service offerings on GCP
- Deploy and run services on managed platforms such as App Engine and Container Engine
- Securely maintain application states with Cloud Storage, Datastore, and Bigtable
- Leverage StackDriver monitoring and debugging to minimize downtime and mitigate issues without impacting users
- Design and implement complex software solutions utilizing Google Cloud
- Integrate with best-in-class big data solutions such as Bigquery, Dataflow, and Pub/Sub

Leave a review - let other readers know what you think

Please share your thoughts on this book with others by leaving a review on the site that you bought it from. If you purchased the book from Amazon, please leave us an honest review on this book's Amazon page. This is vital so that other potential readers can see and use your unbiased opinion to make purchasing decisions, we can understand what our customers think about our products, and our authors can see your feedback on the title that they have worked with Packt to create. It will only take a few minutes of your time, but is valuable to other potential customers, our authors, and Packt. Thank you!

Index

O

one-time password (OTP) 172

P

pay-as-you-go model 6
persistent storage 53, 56, 111
PersistentVolumeClaims (PVC) 112
Platform as a Service (PaaS) 6, 35
preemptible instances 126
Private Google access 91

Q

queries per second (QPS) 62

R

regional external load balancing 92
regional internal load balancing 92
routes 80

S

security keys 186
solid state drives (SSD) 54
Stackdriver debugger 147, 148, 149, 150, 152,
    155, 156
Stackdriver error reporting 142, 144, 145, 146
Stackdriver logging 127, 128, 130, 132, 133,
    135, 136, 137, 138, 139, 140, 142
Stackdriver monitoring 127, 128, 130, 132, 133,
    135, 136, 137, 138
Stackdriver profiler 157, 158, 159, 160, 161, 162

Stackdriver project
    AWS connector project 134
    hosting project 134
    monitored project 134
Stackdriver Trace 162, 164, 165, 166, 167
standard storage 58
stateful application 111
stateless application 111
storage services, Google Cloud Platform (GCP)
    about 8
    cloud BigTable 8
    cloud datastore 8
    cloud spanner 8
    cloud SQL 8
    cloud storage 8
    persistent disk 8
sub-accounts 188

U

Universal 2nd Factor (U2F) 172

V

virtual private cloud (VPC) 25
Virtual Private Networks (VPNs) 9
VM instance
    creating 30, 31, 32
    preemptible 33
VPC network peering 83, 85, 87, 90
VPC networks 74, 76, 78

W

workload 44, 99

CPSIA information can be obtained
at www.ICGtesting.com
Printed in the USA
LVHW021501060119
602928LV00010B/231/P